Confucianism and the Succession Crisis of the Wanli Emperor

"Reacting to the Past" Series

Confucianism and the Succession Crisis of the Wanli Emperor

Third Edition

Mark C. Carnes
Barnard College
Columbia University

Daniel K. Gardner
Smith College

PEARSON
Longman

New York Boston San Francisco
London Toronto Sydney Tokyo Singapore Madrid
Mexico City Munich Paris Cape Town Hong Kong Montreal

Publisher: Priscilla McGeehon
Editorial Assistant: Stephanie Ricotta
Executive Marketing Manager: Sue Westmoreland
Managing Editor: Bob Ginsberg
Production Coordinator: Shafiena Ghani
Senior Cover Design Manager/Designer: Nancy Danahy
Cover Photo: © Getty Images, Inc.
Senior Manufacturing Buyer: Alfred C. Dorsey
Printer and Binder: Phoenix Color Corporation
Cover Printer: Phoenix Color Corporation

Library of Congress Cataloging-in-Publication Data

CIP data is on file with the Library of Congress

Please visit our website at http://www.ablongman.com

ISBN 0-321-33230-X

1 2 3 4 5 6 7 8 9 10—PBT—07 06 05 04

Contents

Confucianism and the Succession Crisis of the Wanli Emperor

Key Names, Old and New Spellings, with Simplified Pronunciation

Note on Romanization of Chinese: In this book we use what has become the standard system of transliteration from Chinese, called *pinyin*. The older system, Wade-Giles, is used in Ray Huang's *1587: A Year of No Significance*. When using reference and scholarly works in the library, you will generally find that recent works, those from the past decade or two, use *pinyin*, while older works use Wade-Giles. It can be more troublesome than this, however, as even today, some scholars--though fewer and fewer--continue to use the Wade-Giles system.

Old transliteration   New transliteration

Wade-Giles (old style)	Pinyin (new style)	Relation	Pronunciation
Wan-li	Wanli	Emperor	WAN-LEE
Chang Chü-cheng	Zhang Juzheng	First Grand Secretary, 1572-1582	JANG JOO-JENG
Lady Wang	same	Mother of first-born son, Changluo	WANG
Lady Cheng	Lady Zheng	Mother of second-born son, Changxun	JENG
Ch'ang-lo	Changluo	First-born son	CHANG-LWO
Ch'ang-hsün	Changxun	Second-born son	CHANG-SCHWUN
Feng Pao	Feng Bao	Head palace eunuch during Zhang era	FUNG BAO
Shen Shih-hsing	Shen Shixing	First grand secretary after Zhang [who, for purposes of game, is presumed to have died in 1587]	SHEN SURE-SHING
Hai Jui	Hai Rui	Traditionalist and moralist	HI-RAY
Confucius		Founder of Confucian school	
Peking (postal spelling)	Beijing	Capital of empire	

The Exam

You stare at the words. They **look** familiar and the question follows the usual pattern. You know you have copied that particular analect scores of times—no, hundreds. You have recited it from memory. You have studied and memorized the standard commentary on it by Zhu Xi as well. Your Cram-Book included full discussion of this very analect, suggesting what a model answer for it would be. You had even gone over and over it with your tutor last winter. And yet now, as you scrutinize the words, you're drawing a blank.

You close your eyes, hoping to blink away the fog. When you open them, the characters have grown larger and their forms more distinct, but still no more meaningful. The pressure of the examination has you confused and afraid. You begin to remember the legion of stories of examination candidates haunted in their cells by ghosts and fox fairies who come to settle old scores; you even remember tell of highly promising candidates dropping dead of fear in their cells in the middle of the night. Now you start to wonder: is the confusion and fear you're feeling "examination retribution" for some wrong you committed? Your mind recounts all sorts of mistakes and errors in judgment you've made in the last few years alone. You become fixated now on one particular occasion—the time that, professing your love to the poor peasant girl from neighboring Bailian village, you took advantage of her innocence, and then never saw her again. Will her ghost—or her father's ghost perhaps—be paying you a visit? You sit up straight and remind yourself that you must not panic. You must concentrate and put any thoughts of ghosts and fox-fairies entirely out of your mind.

You are sweating, both from fear and the humid heat of the evening, so you slip out of your gown. Perspiration has stained your underwear, bought especially for the examination. You think of the stories in the academy about the "Cheat Shorts," embroidered in tiny stitches with texts of all Four Books, including the *Analects* and Zhu Xi's commentary. Students had joked about this, but you noticed some of the laughter had been forced. One teacher, it was rumored, could provide such underwear for a small fee. Now you wonder: why didn't you approach him? You begin to think back on all the many years you've devoted to preparing for the civil service examinations. You think back too on the innumerable sacrifices your family has made to enable you to live the examination life. You **are** desperate to pass, both for your sake and your family's; yet cheating by any means would make a total lie and mockery of the Confucian principles you've given your life to all these years.

Perhaps the significance of the analect will all come back if you begin to write. You sit at the desk and arrange the paper, smoothing it with your hand. Its glossy perfection shows that it is official paper. Whatever your score, the exam will be kept in the archives. You check the bristles on the goat-hair brush, best for the initial marks. You stir the black ink. "Your first stroke must be firm and strong," your calligraphy teacher had said. "An essay is like a beautiful house. It must rest upon firm timbers." Then he would tell you, as if you had not heard the story a hundred times, about how he would have been awarded a jinshi or "presented scholar" degree had his paper not been smudged, or so he learned afterwards. Who had told him, he never said. "A slovenly person cannot comprehend the Way of the Master," he admonished, arching his eyebrows.

But his warnings never troubled you. On the contrary, you had always excelled at calligraphy. Even as a young child you liked the shapes of the characters and the varying textures of the brush-strokes. When you were five (you'd heard the story often, always retold with novel embellishments) you dipped your fingers in the fish sauce at dinner and trailed them along the bottom of an empty bowl. "Stop playing with your food," your mother had said. But one day your oldest brother noticed that, as you smeared the sauce in the bowl, you kept glancing at the tea shop across the street. Then he realized that you were copying the characters on the sign.

The next day your mother walked with you to visit Great Uncle Hong, who lived beyond the river. While you played with your cousins, they conferred over tea. Then he took you into his study and sat you at his desk. He said that you were to play a game with him. He gave you a small brush and a pot with ink. He drew a character, and said it was a kind of picture. He gave it a name. Then he moved the picture around, so that the names moved, too. He used the "moving names" to tell a story. Next he asked you to copy his picture-names, and then to tell your own story. He smiled, and encouraged you to say more. You stayed overnight. After breakfast, your mother explained that she was to go back home. "You are to stay and play with Uncle Hong, games with the brush and ink."

Several weeks later she returned with your father. That evening, relatives from the entire clan came to Uncle Hong's. You had never met most of them. After dinner he told you that he wanted to play the same games, but this time everyone crowded around to watch. Some of the men scowled, and the others were serious. You were fearful and began to chew on your knuckles. But Uncle smiled, and you began to play. In a few moments you became absorbed in the game and forgot about the others; then you noticed that the room was still. You glanced up, and all of the faces were staring at you. Your father looked as if he had been rattled by thunder. Uncle Hong tapped your arm, and you resumed the game.

After you had gone to bed, you overheard male voices, some of them loud. Then you fell asleep. In the morning, your mother called you "My clever son!" and smiled. She explained that you were now to stay and study with Uncle Hong all summer.

In the fall you returned home and were sent to study with a respected and learned tutor in the village. He was an old man, a former civil servant. He taught calligraphy and drummed more characters into your head. By your seventh birthday, you could recognize and even write several thousand characters. By age eleven, you had memorized most of the Four Books, including the *Analects*. By age twelve, you wrote poetry and began studying the *bagu* [eight-legged] essay style required on the exams. You were also introduced to the officially-sanctioned commentaries on the Four Books, all by Zhu Xi.

That year, when you visited Uncle Hong for the first time in several years, your knowledge of the Four Books, and especially your ability to recite from memory all of the commentaries on the Four Books, impressed him deeply. Uncle Hong took the occasion to explain about Great Grandfather Li, long dead. Nearly seventy years ago, Li had won a small piece of land in a gambling game. He called that land the "Scholar's Plot," and kept the money it generated in a locked box. When a true prodigy appeared in the family, the money would be used for his education to enable him to compete for the civil service examinations. If he passed, he could become a provincial official and cast fame and perhaps fortune upon the entire clan. After Great Grandfather Li died, the box was passed down to the oldest male relation of the clan. "You are our hope," Hong told you, and then his smile broadened. "No, my son. You are our destiny."

The recollection of Uncle Hong's face reassures you. You put your brush between your thumb and third finger, dip it in the ink, and raise it, checking that the axis of the paper is in line with the first arm motion.

Then you see it. A drop of ink is quivering at the end of the goat-hairs. Your hand is trembling! You try to force it to be still, but the ink forms a large blob, and wobbles. You will dribble ink upon the paper and ruin it. You thrust the brush back into the ink.

Then you stare at the exam question. Again, nothing!

You stand to stretch your legs, but you move too quickly and feel dizzy. You try to force the dizziness away by taking a few steps in each direction, but the cubicle is small, smaller than it had seemed when you first came in. You hear the candidate urinating into a pot in the adjacent cubicle. He can function normally; he is unconcerned. You hear your stomach churning. You glance at your pot. What if you throw up or lose control of your bowels? What will the student in the next cubicle think? Will he call for help? Will the monitor disqualify you? The exams won't be given again for three years.

You have been pushing the Bad Thought away, but can do so no longer. You cannot write a word. You cannot read the text. When the list of successful candidates is posted, your name will appear nowhere on it. You will fail.

What will you tell Uncle Hong? Your mother? The members of your clan? The village people who had lined the street and cheered as you set out with your father in brand-new clothes to walk to the provincial capital? How can you explain that you forgot everything you had learned over the past twelve years?

You sit down and put your head on the desk. It begins to swirl, slowly at first, and then faster. **This is not happening to you!**

A tinkling sound, and you stir.

"Your tea, Honored Master." Your servant of many years, holding a tray, looks down, averting her eyes.

You see the papers upon the table—memorials to the Ministry of Rites, a statement of imperial accounts with builders, the usual state business. You glance around. There is no cubicle. You are in your elegant garden study. Your favorite rock, a towering slab both rough and jagged, contrasts with the perfectly smooth brickwork of the courtyard. Fish, dappled orange and white, wriggle in the pond above blue-grey rocks. Yin and yang, dark and light, rough and smooth, wet and dry—cosmic truths arrayed in exquisite form, all by your design.

You had not failed that provincial exam. When the results were posted, your name was on the top. Three months later you went to Beijing to sit for the metropolitan exam, hoping to win the coveted "presented scholars" degree. Not only did you win the degree, but you placed among the top three, and so won a prestigious posting to the Hanlin Academy. There you specialized in writing the emperor's edicts. So impressed had the emperor become with your literary talent and sound political judgment that last year he elevated you to the most powerful body in the land, the Grand Secretariat.

Provincial officials erected great stele commemorating your achievements at the burial site of Uncle Hong and your parents. When you find time to return to your ancestral home, borne by a half-dozen men upon a black-lacquered sedan chair, the entire province turns out to cheer your passage.

No, you did not fail—ever.

As you look about your garden, a shaft of light illuminates the tracery of bamboo leaves. Yet repose eludes you. Why, you wonder, does the Exam Nightmare still come?

Tomorrow morning, you have an audience with the emperor himself. His Majesty is extremely anxious. A number of critical issues now confront the empire—flooding, "barbarian" incursions, and insufficient state revenues, among others. He seeks your advice and that of other advisors in the Grand Secretariat. He knows that if he doesn't successfully address the various problems, he risks losing the Mandate. And looming over all China, like a great storm cloud, is the issue of which of his sons will succeed the emperor.

The burden on your shoulders is great. In just a few hours you will have a personal audience with the Son of Heaven himself, who is looking to you for answers. You must not fail him, nor Confucius, nor those twenty thousand civil servants who look to the Hanlin for guidance. If you fail, you will disgrace not just yourself, but also Uncle Hong and your parents. If you fail, you may even endanger the survival of the Ming and the well-being of all under heaven.

Introduction: The Historical Context

The year is 1587. The place is the Grand Secretariat in the Forbidden City in Beijing. The Wanli emperor has provoked a crisis: he has refused to designate his first-born son, Changluo, now six, as his successor. Wanli has shown little interest in the boy and still less in his mother, Lady Wang. His refusal to designate Changluo as his successor is momentous because in recent months Wanli has just had a son by his favorite concubine, Lady Zheng. The infant's name is Changxun. Changxun is Wanli's third-born son (his second son died in infancy). Many in the Grand Secretariat worry that the Wanli emperor, perhaps influenced by Lady Zheng, will eventually name Changxun as his successor.

The Grand Secretariat is the most distinguished and influential body in Ming government, a sort of informal, collective prime-ministership which directly advises the emperor. Becoming a Grand Secretary is unthinkable to most mortals; a person first has to win an appointment to the Hanlin Academy, the agency in the Forbidden City responsible for drafting and editing the writings of the emperor. Appointments to the Hanlin Academy go only to the most promising and successful candidates in the civil service examinations (more on the exams later). Once in the Hanlin, an especially talented academician might someday come to the attention of the emperor and be given an appointment to the Grand Secretariat. Grand Secretaries, the number of which was never fixed (though fewer than ten was common), normally hold their position for life. As Grand Secretaries they retain their official association with the Hanlin Academy.

The Grand Secretaries are anxious about the succession issue. Some believe that passing over Changluo, the first-born, would represent a violation of Confucian precepts that insist on the privilege of age and sex. Young people are to defer to their elders; young siblings are to defer to older ones. Women are to defer to men; the Ruler of All Under Heaven, bound though he may be by ideological constraints, need defer to no one, and especially not to a woman. Social order and the stability of the empire depend on these hierarchical precepts. If the emperor himself does not adhere to them, why should his subjects?

Others believe that it is precisely the place of the ruler to exercise his imperial judgment about which of his sons will make for the best ruler, about who will care most genuinely for the welfare of the people. In their view, shouldn't virtue be the main criterion in the selection of an heir? And who knows the character of his sons, the possible heirs to the throne, better than the emperor himself? Didn't the legendary sage-ruler Yao, according to the Confucian Classic, the *Book of History*, pass over his own son, deeming him unworthy, and place instead on the throne Shun, a man of humble origins, but exceeding virtue (see "Canon of Yao" in packet)? Further, if Confucian precepts require the young to defer to their elders and women to defer to men, must not the people defer to the wishes of the Son of Heaven? Do not the hierarchical principles of Confucius require all subjects, even Hanlin academicians and the Grand Secretaries in the Hanlin, to show the emperor dutiful obedience?

A faction of Grand Secretaries has emerged in support of Lady Wang and her boy, while another faction supports Wanli. In the background of the factional dispute lie some of the most crucial issues of Confucian morality and governance. How can so immense an empire be ruled if the fundamental beliefs that hold it together, sanctified by the Heavenly mandate, are neglected by the Son of Heaven himself? How can the Confucian principles that cement families, clans, regions, and the empire as a whole be sustained if the emperor himself neglects them? Exactly as the father must provide both the example and substance of family governance, so, too, the emperor must behave in relation to the people, his subjects.

Others contend, however, that obedience—to elders, to fathers, and to the emperor—is a cornerstone of Confucianism. How can an immense empire, consisting of several hundred million people, be ruled if people decide for themselves which laws are to be obeyed? How can children upbraid their parents, and the young chastise those who have been ennobled by age? Can the judgment of the emperor, virtuous father and mother of all under Heaven, be readily called into question without destabilizing the entire political order?

While the dispute has created considerable tension among the Grand Secretaries, indeed, shaping much of their debate over other practical matters facing the empire, the naming of the heir-apparent in the end rests entirely with one person, the Wanli emperor. Wanli lives in magnificent splendor (and near-complete isolation) in the vast grounds of the Forbidden City. There he associates with three main groups of people: 1) about a dozen members of the Grand Secretariat, who comprise the top level of the Confucian-educated bureaucracy. (The Grand Secretaries serve as part of the inner court; the rest of the official bureaucracy, numbering some 22,000 scholars, constitutes the so-called outer court, at much greater distance from and with far less influence on the emperor. The overwhelming dominance of the Grand Secretariat results in an uneasy, sometime hostile relationship with members of the outer court, who tend to view the Grand Secretaries as personal agents of the emperor and occasional collaborators with eunuchs at the inner court). 2) 3,000 palace women, who perform all sorts of chores and even serve as consorts and concubines of the emperor and other members of the imperial family; and 3) thousands of eunuchs, persons either who were castrated as punishment for a crime or who as adolescents castrated themselves in the hope of gaining employment in the Forbidden City. Eunuchs have been a presence at the inner court since the Qin dynasty (221 B.C.E.-206 B.C.E.). Because they are unable to reproduce, they can be trusted in the vicinity of the emperor's personal consorts and concubines; and because they have no progeny, they are thought to be free of scheming to enrich their children and descendents.

Though most eunuchs are employed in menial tasks, some have attended special schools and attained literary skills equal to the top-ranking Confucian bureaucrats. Because of their presence in the inner court in such close proximity to the emperor, some win the confidence, even the friendship, of the emperor and thus are entrusted by him with important tasks in imperial administration and statecraft. This, of course, greatly dismays members of the Confucian bureaucracy. These civil officials, including some members of the Grand Secretariat, tend to feel only contempt for eunuchs: not only have eunuchs not won civil service degrees and thus the *legitimate* right to conduct official business, they have also committed the most unfilial, most un-Confucian act in dismembering the bodies bequeathed them by their ancestors and curtailing their reproductive capabilities. As a result, a very uneasy tension exists between the eunuchs and the bureaucrats of the inner court and the outer court; yet these bureaucrats, even the most powerful in the Grand Secretariat, ally themselves with eunuchs when they find it to their advantage.

Game Context: The Historical Record and Counterfactual Premises, After 1587

The game is based on the actual historical context as outlined in Ray Huang,'s *1587: A Year of No Significance* (Yale) **up to a point**. That is, everything mentioned in the book up to and through 1587 has really occurred and may be cited as fact.

Though focused on that single year, Huang's book includes mention of events and actions that occur in later years. For the purposes of this game, these events and actions **have not happened and may not happen**. Students can assume that the subsequent historical forces cited in the book may still have validity (for example: the persistence of troubles with barbarians in the north and northwest, or of banditry in Shandong, or of Yellow River flooding); students should not assume that any particular barbarian invasion or act of banditry actually occurred.

The game also includes several counterfactual premises:

> First, that First Grand Secretary Shen Shixing has just died, uneventfully and of natural causes; the Wanli emperor will soon name a new one. [In fact, Shen remained in office for many years.]

> Second, that the Wanli emperor has agreed to meet regularly with his Grand Secretariat. Whether this points to a significant change in his attitude remains to be seen.

> Third, the Grand Secretariat's audiences with the emperor are not held at sunrise, and the Grand Secretaries are not obliged to stand throughout. Other ritual prescriptions may be required. These will be spelled out at the outset by the First Grand Secretary.

BASIC OUTLINE OF THE GAME

The classroom will become the palace room where the academicians in the Grand Secretariat have their audiences with the Wanli emperor. Every student in the game will be a member of the Grand Secretariat. There is one exception: the Wanli emperor himself.

Wanli Emperor

The game will begin with the selection of the Wanli emperor. The selection process may be random, or it may be determined in some other manner by the Gamemaster. Students who served in leadership roles or especially active factions in a previous game may be barred from being considered for the emperor position.

The empire's land is the emperor's land; it belongs entirely to him. The emperor has the power of life and death over everyone and everything. His power is unchecked by law, as there exists no constitution. It is, however, naturally constrained by ideological beliefs (often associated with Confucian teachings) and practical politics.

The Wanli emperor's first task is to choose a First Grand Secretary to replace the recently deceased Shen (see counterfactual premise #2). This decision must first be approved by the Gamemaster, who may insist that the FGS not be chosen from the same faction as that of Wanli in a previous game. The decision will be announced at the beginning of the next class.

The First Grand Secretary

The First Grand Secretary serves as the leader of the Grand Secretariat; he is the top-ranking official of the most powerful bureaucratic body in the empire. [The Grand Secretariat is loosely analogous to that of a modern cabinet.] The First Grand Secretary is the emperor's chief adviser and his intermediary with the rest of the Grand Secretaries. The First Grand Secretary's power is entirely derived from the emperor, whose signature possesses the force of law on all decrees and laws. Because the First Grand Secretary controls the flow of information, and tax revenues and expenditures, he has considerable **effective** power.

In addition, the First Grand Secretary organizes each day's sessions and tends to preside over them as well, though, of course, Wanli may do whatever he wishes. The First Grand Secretary directs the activities of the other Grand Secretaries, each of whom is attached to a major ministry of government. The First Grand Secretary can oblige them to undertake whatever work he would like to see done.

When the First Grand Secretary has been chosen, he receives his role sheet.

The Grand Secretaries

All the remaining students will be members of the Grand Secretariat. Each has excelled at progressively difficult and intense examinations that test literary skills and knowledge of the Confucian classics. Their skills in reading and writing are indispensable in a territorially far-flung empire that is held together by paper: tax payments, accounts of government expenditures (for armies and navies, flood control, bandit and pirate suppression, police forces, ceremonial performance, and so on), imperial decrees, personnel reports, and all manners of memoranda. Their shared literacy and, still more, their shared knowledge of a particular body of Confucian texts, including the *Analects,* make them and all civil officials in China a fellowship of sorts, one where general understanding and acceptance of core Confucian values are assumed.

THE IMPASSE

A large number of Grand Secretaries (perhaps the majority) oppose the Wanli emperor's hesitation to name his first-born son (Changluo) as his imperial successor. They oppose as well his continued emotional dependence on Lady Zheng, whose sponsorship of her son, Changxun, seems a foregone conclusion. Many Secretaries want, first, that the Wanli emperor name Changluo as imperial successor, and second, that the Wanli demote Lady Zheng as imperial consort. The Wanli seems reluctant to do either.

This concern over succession is only one of many issues facing the Grand Secretariat. Like officials of earlier dynasties, they are concerned too with how best to deal with the "barbarian" presence to the North and Northwest. Throughout the Ming period Mongols, Manchus, and Tanguts have periodically encroached on China's borders. Some civil officials, including some in the Grand Secretariat itself, believe that more active attention must be paid to the growing threat of these "barbarian" peoples. They are mindful that it was not too long ago that the Mongols successfully conquered the whole of China and established the Yuan dynasty (1279-1368). Only with the Ming founder's defeat of the Mongol regime was the Yuan brought to an end. But even into the Ming the threat continues; as recently as 1550 a raiding party of Mongols breached the defenses of the capital and looted the city of Beijing.

Another serious matter for the Grand Secretariat is the control of the Yellow River. In recent decades it has been prone to flooding, bringing famine and severe hardship to the peasantry in North China. Famine and hardship, in turn, encourage a rise in banditry. Can the river be controlled? If so, how? Will more taxes be required? Are the officials in the area of the Yellow River doing an effective job? Could they be doing a better job? What role should the emperor play?

Banditry too has become a problem in almost every province in the empire and piracy plagues the southeast coastal region. Why? What accounts for the spread of this sort of social and economic disorder? What is the effect on the people of the empire? Is it possible to control better the banditry and piracy? What measures could be taken?

As ever, the Grand Secretariat is deeply worried about taxation and revenue as well. More revenue might enable the government to provide stronger defense against "barbarian" incursions, to deal more decisively with banditry and piracy, and to provide effective irrigation control. But how best to raise the revenue? Should the monopoly on the salt industry be continued? Has it been effective? Should the government impose monopolies on other industries, such as iron, liquor, and tea? Ever since the Han dynasty, governments have resorted to monopolies in times of fiscal crisis. But government monopolies have always caused great controversy, not just among the people, but within the bureaucracy itself. The record of the first such controversy, the *Discourses on Salt and Iron* (see excerpts in this packet), was drawn up in the first century B.C.E. and ever since has inspired those on both sides of the issue.

Finally, the examination system continues to be a source of concern. Is it the most efficient means of recruiting the most effective officials? Do the Confucian texts prepare one well to serve as an official? Is the system truly meritocratic? Are the best men being found? In fact, should the present examination system be entirely replaced by a system of recommendation (SATs vs. letters of recommendation)? The form and content of the examination system have been debated for centuries. The emperor wants the Grand Secretariat to consider the matter and make recommendations.

The tension in the Grand Secretariat over the issue of succession is to some extent a product of the disagreement among the Grand Secretaries over some of these more practical matters. That is, the factionalism that develops around the first-born and the third-born is generated, in some measure, by the different political stances and affiliations of the Grand Secretaries. To put it another way, the political and philosophical differences of the Grand Secretaries cannot readily be disentangled from their dispute over succession to Wanli.

The Grand Secretaries advise the emperor by presenting papers to him. When these are delivered from the podium as a formal address, these memorials are published—copied by scribes and transmitted throughout the Ming bureaucracy. If the emperor or the First Grand Secretary chooses to respond, these, too, are published and distributed to the bureaucracy.

CONCLUSION

If, during the last session of the game, a great many members of the Grand Secretariat publish memorials critical of the Wanli emperor and his policies, that will serve as a strong signal to the Confucian bureaucracy throughout the empire that the emperor has lost much of his moral authority. Some bureaucrats will be confused; they will wonder: has he gone astray, has he lost his virtue and right to rule? Others might even see it as their duty to resign. If the Confucian bureaucracy does begin to abandon the emperor, his effective rule will come to an end.

At this point, the Wanli emperor must dismiss his First Grand Secretary and name his chief adversary as the new First Grand Secretary; Wanli must also order that Lady Zheng move far away from Beijing. In this event, Wanli must at the same time announce that he has named Changluo (#1 son) as successor. These concessions are necessary to regain the confidence of the Grand Secretaries and the bureaucracy and the support of the empire. Otherwise he risks losing the Mandate of Heaven forever.

If in the end, however, the weight of opinion in the Grand Secretariat is not critical, and does not go against Wanli, the emperor's chosen First Grand Secretary may remain in power and Wanli may continue as in the past. [What constitutes the "weight" of opinion is a complicated matter known fully only to the Gamemaster.]

Some Grand Secretaries are, at the outset of the game, undecided on the main issues, and especially on the issue of succession. They need guidance. They will likely determine the outcome of the game.

Rules

The emperor sets them all, although his powers are in fact circumscribed both by the teachings of Confucianism (see the section of this packet on that subject) and by the power of the civil bureaucracy. For instance, he can order the execution of anyone in the empire—even a top-ranking official—and can assume that that order will be carried out immediately.

Of course, emperors had always been loath to impose any sort of corporal punishment on civil officials; after all, these were men who wielded significant power and who, because of their success in the competitive examinations, were held in high public esteem. However, that would change with the first emperor of the Ming, Hongwu (r. 1368-1398). A commoner with little education, Hongwu viewed all of his officials with considerable suspicion; they were a threat to his authority. Indeed, he is reported to have executed thousands of his officials, including his own prime minister, for behavior he regarded as disrespectful or treasonous. To be sure, later emperors of the Ming were more cautious, and yet the tradition of corporal punishment of officials persisted throughout the dynasty.

For an emperor to execute civil officials, men thought to be models of Confucian morality, there were risks, however. Perhaps the Mandate of Heaven would be withdrawn from the dynasty; perhaps cosmic displeasure would give rise to floods and plagues and all manner of calamities; or perhaps critics might band together in secret societies and even rise up in armed rebellion. While the emperor may at times be obliged to take extreme measures—good parents must sometimes chastise rebellious children—it is important, even essential, in such instances that the emperor's rationale be grounded in Confucian precepts and disseminated in writing.

If the emperor seeks to make any pronouncements of a legal character (e.g., the establishment of a new tax system, a change in the civil service examination system, the punishment of a civil servant), they must be in writing and bear his signature. These documents should be filed with the Gamemaster for safekeeping in the imperial archives.

All lectures or memorials that are delivered to the emperor will be copied, published, and disseminated throughout the realm (via class website, if one has been established).

As in all other games, students have the right to approach the podium and to take a place in line to express their views. Whether Wanli will recognize the speaker is another matter. But once a Grand Secretariat is at the podium and has begun a speech, the emperor or First Grand Secretary can interrupt only to enforce time rules.

Special rules

BEHAVIOR OF EMPEROR DURING AUDIENCES WITH ACADEMICIANS

Although the emperor has the nominal power of life and death over all inhabitants of China, there are nonetheless certain constraints on his own behavior. For instance, during formal presentations by members of the Grand Secretariat, the emperor must be attentive and respectful. The symbolism of the audiences is clear: the academicians embody the knowledge and wisdom of Confucius; whatever the Emperor thinks of the views of the academicians, he must not interrupt during each academician's formal presentation. If the emperor nods off or ceases to exhibit respect during the presentations, or if he sits with crossed legs, the academician delivering the paper is obliged by ritual to instruct the emperor to pay attention, to sit straight, and to uncross his legs. After being upbraided, the emperor is obliged by ritual to apologize for his unseemly behavior. After a formal presentation and during the discussions that may follow, the emperor is free to comment sharply and critically upon what has been said.

PUNISHMENT OF GRAND SECRETARIES

Wanli can exile a member of the Grand Secretariat or even have him put to death. Either action, however, as noted above, would be profoundly unsettling; unless it was justified by Confucian precepts, it would likely put his legitimacy as a true Confucian ruler at risk.

Historical Context: The Ming Dynasty

For the preceding two thousand years, China has vacillated between periods of decentralized rule, when central authority has dissolved and local lords have imposed their will (and established some local order), and periods of strong dynastic domination, when central government has established effective control over the whole of China (recognizing, of course, that Chinese boundaries have shifted dramatically over the millennia). Some of the dynasties you may well come across in your reading are: the Zhou (1050 B.C.E.-221 B.C.E.) and its era known as the "Warring States" period (403-221); the Qin (221-206 B.C.E.); the Han (206 B.C.E.-220 A.D.); the Tang (618-907); the Song (960-1279); the Yuan [the Mongols] (1279-1368); the Ming (1368-1644); and the Qing [the Manchus] (1644-1912).

The central issues of the Ming Dynasty—economic, political, administrative, military, and the like—are discussed later in this packet in Chapter 8 of *China: Tradition and Transformation,* edited by John K. Fairbank and Edwin O. Reischauer. This chapter provides the context that makes intelligible Ray Huang's book, which focuses on a single year during the reign of the Wanli, one of the last Ming emperors. Students should read this chapter before plunging into Huang.

1563   Wanli born, first son of Ming Emperor Longqing.

1572   Longqing dies; Wanli (age nine) succeeds him.

1572   Zhang Juzheng becomes first grand secretary: embarks on efficiency crusade.

1577   Zhang's father dies; Wanli orders Zhang to forego the usual 27-month mourning period; criticisms of Zhang—and emperor—mount.

1578   Wanli marries Xiaotuan, in response to mother's desire to have many grandchildren; they have daughter; Wanli ignores Xiaotuan.

1581   Wanli impregnates chambermaid; **Wanli's first son, named Changluo, is born (1582)**. The chambermaid is promoted to Consort, and is now addressed as Lady Wang.

1582   Zhang Juzheng dies; quickly discredited. Shen soon becomes first grand secretary.

1583   Wanli falls in love with one of his nine new concubines, named Lady Zheng, who quickly becomes his favorite.

1586   **Wanli has son (Changxun) by Lady Zheng;** Wanli insists that Lady Zheng be named Imperial consort (higher rank than "consort"). Note: The imperial consort was a public office, inferior in rank only to the empress (emperor's mother) and ahead of all other concubines, including Lady Wang. Bureaucratic resistance to this action ensues. The chief issue: that Changxun, the number three son, will usurp the rights of the eldest son, thereby undermining a fundamental principle of Confucian rectitude and order on which social and dynastic order is based.

Confucius and Confucianism

CONFUCIUS AND HIS TIME

Master Kong or Kong Fuzi (551-479 B.C.E.) was born in the state of Lu in eastern China (present-day Shandong) into a family of the lower ranks of the nobility. He lived during what is known as the Eastern Zhou period (770-256), a time when imperial rule was more of a fiction than a reality. Zhou emperors had but little territory under their own direct control and, consequently, only a small, token army. Real power rested in the hands of feudal lords ruling the many regional states; although nominally under the control of the Zhou Emperor, these lords were *de facto* independent rulers who regularly waged war against one another. In the early years of the Eastern Zhou, these wars tended to be ceremonial in character, governed by a highly ritualistic code of behavior, but by Confucius' time they had become deadly affairs. By the close of the fifth century B.C.E. it was not unusual for a war between feudal states to involve hundreds of thousands of troops and last for years at time. The populations of whole states were routinely decimated. This period of uninterrupted warfare, known aptly as the "warring states era," lasted for nearly 200 years (403-221 B.C.E.) and only came to an end when the state of Qin (221-206 B.C.E.) conquered all its rival states and established itself as a new dynastic power.

In short, the Eastern Zhou was a rather bleak world, characterized by political disunity and constant war. It was into this world that Confucius was born. Desperate to set the world aright, to return China to its earlier greatness of the Western Zhou (1050-770 B.C.E.), Confucius proceeded from one feudal state to another, hoping to gain the ear— and employment—of a feudal ruler, who might then put his political advice into practice. He fervently believed that his place was in the world of politics. Except for a brief stint in his native state of Lu, Confucius was unsuccessful in finding political employment. Deeply disappointed, he turned to teaching, hoping perhaps that his disciples might in the end be successful where he had failed. It is in this manner that Confucius became China's first professional teacher.

But Confucius was not alone in his efforts to address the political and social problems of his day. Philosophers of all varieties began to appear, each believing that his ideas could bring political unity and cultural greatness back to China, the Middle Kingdom. With Confucius then, we have the start of what is commonly called the golden age of Chinese philosophy, a time when a "hundred schools" of thought prospered. Daoists, legalists, militarists, diplomatists, Mohists, yin/yangists—just to name a few—arose. Their messages were quite different, but they all aimed to provide answers to the problems facing a fractured China characterized by serious warfare among the feudal states. Thus, out of the political disunity and the social instability of the Eastern Zhou emerged one of the most vital intellectual movements in Chinese, and perhaps world, history.

During the Zhou period then, Confucianism was but one among many contending schools of thought. Only with time would Confucianism come to achieve something of a privileged status in China. This was made possible by the efforts of his disciples and, in turn, their disciples. Together, these two generations of disciples of "the Master" collected together his teachings as he had uttered them to students and edited them into the book known as *Lunyu*, conventionally translated as the *Analects*. While scholars have sometimes argued about which "books" of the *Analects* may be most "authentic," or most likely to represent the core teachings of the Master himself, the text as a whole, in its twenty books, has been treated by the Chinese tradition itself as representing the true teachings of Confucius. That is, this small classic has for millennia been embraced by Chinese readers as the words of the Master.

CONFUCIAN PHILOSOPHY

The Master's interests were focused on the world of humankind, the everyday world. What mattered to him were the relationships between and among human beings. How can human beings best relate to one another? What makes for good human relations? What makes for a good person? What role can and should government play in bringing about a world of harmonious social relations? These are the questions that preoccupied him. Confucius never speaks of a monotheistic God, a creator, a will external to and responsible for the universe. In his world view, then, a person's primary relationship cannot be to his or her God, his or her creator, as it has been in western religious traditions, but rather the primary relationship is to his fellow human beings, and especially to his family, to whom he owes everything.

Major Concepts of Confucianism

The emphasis that Confucius places on the social, the interrelational, and the moral is reflected in all of the major concepts introduced in the *Analects*:

Junzi **or Gentleman**: Confucius would have all men aspire to become gentlemen, men who know how to conduct themselves *as they should* in all of their interactions with others. The Chinese word *junzi* literally means the "son of the ruler," a term that until the time of Confucius had referred to the hereditary aristocracy, those born of a certain class. This was the highest position one could hold in society; it was assumed that men of this class would comport themselves appropriately. Ingeniously, Confucius took the term and gave it a strongly moral dimension, arguing that the *junzi* is one who is morally superior, who has learned how to behave well in all situations in life. For him, *junzi* is not a mark of birth or limited to heredity, but is a status, to be sure a superior status, attainable by anyone.

Li **or Ritual**: Here again Confucius takes a word that had long been part of the Chinese cultural tradition and gives it a different emphasis. *Li* is a difficult word to translate well, as "ritual" is something that in the west we tend to associate with a sacred place or sacred time. Indeed, this is largely what *li* had been prior to Confucius, that is, the rituals or rites associated with ancestral ceremonies, burials, mourning, and the like. For Confucius, *li* are to be found everywhere. Rituals, ceremonies, etiquette, and customs—all possible translations of *li*— govern our daily lives, and all of our relationships. There is a set of *li* that governs the relationship between parent and child, a set that governs the relationship between ruler and subject, a set that governs the relationship between friend and friend, and a set that governs the relationship between student and teacher. In other words, the secular world, the everyday, is characterized by the performance of *li*. How we greet each other, how we speak to each other, how we dress—these too are for Confucius a matter of ritual or custom. The proper performance of them by all of us makes, in his view, for a world that is fully harmonious and fully human. The performance of such ritual, the proper performance that is, is what separates human beings from other species.

***Ren* or Benevolence**: *Ren* can be variously translated as benevolence, humaneness, or goodness, and for Confucius it is the consummate virtue, the one that embodies all others. The Chinese character for *ren* is illuminating, consisting of two components, one meaning person and one meaning two. That is, one can be *ren* only in relation to another. A person of *ren* will in all situations treat others as they should be treated. This requires that one be empathetic, capable of "not imposing on others what you yourself do not desire." Thus benevolence cannot be realized in isolation but only in interaction with others.

***De* or Virtue**: *De* is the virtue or power possessed by one who has brought total perfection to the practice of *ren* and *li*. It is a power that illuminates outwardly from within, manifesting itself readily to others. Some have likened it to an almost magical charisma, which through a moral force exercises a power to attract and serve as an example for others.

***Dao* or Way**: The *Analects* goes on at length about the Way, literally, road, path, method, or way. For Confucius, it would seem to mean something like "the Way of the ancients," that is, the Way followed by the great sages of the past, especially Kings Wen and Wu of the early Zhou and the Duke of Zhou. It was this Way that made for the perfectly harmonious social and political order of the early Zhou period. Of course it was a moral Way, one where people embraced and practiced the *li* appropriate to their status. When the Way prevails on earth, in the world of human beings, the Way of human beings accords with the Way of heaven and perfect harmony prevails.

Paradigmatic Relationships: Morality for Confucius is relational and pragmatic. One is to behave as is appropriate to the particular circumstances and relationship at hand. There is a way to treat the emperor, a way to treat a father, a way to treat a husband, a way to treat an elder brother, and a way to treat a friend. One has to know the proper *li* governing the circumstances and relationship and practice it with authentic feeling. Confucius's paradigmatic relationships are all hierarchical:

Emperor / subject
Father / son
Husband / wife
Elder brother / younger brother
Elder friend / younger friend.

It is essential to an understanding of Confucianism to appreciate that while the main relationships are hierarchical, between superior and inferior, the obligations are reciprocal, flowing in two directions. Yes, the subject must show obedience to the ruler, but the ruler, to be a true ruler, is required to treat the subject with the paternal affection a father would show his children. The wife should be loyal and obedient to her husband, but the husband, to be a true husband, must care for his wife and treat her with respect.

On Spirits and Ancestors

In 11.12 (Book XI, number 12) of the *Analects* a disciple asks Confucius how the spirits of the dead and the gods are to be served. The Master responds, "You are not able even to serve man. How can you serve the spirits?" This has often— and wrongly—been read as "evidence" of an agnosticism on the Master's part. The remark surely does not constitute evidence for such a claim, but rather underscores that for Confucius there was a clear set of priorities: first serve the world of the living, the world of fellow human beings, and then consider the spirit world.

Throughout the *Analects* Confucius shows an acceptance of existing beliefs in a spirit world; but he is especially invested in the belief in the spirits of one's own ancestors. The cult of worshipping one's ancestors pre-dates Confucius by at least a millennium. The custom had been formalized under the previous Shang dynasty, as evidenced by writing on the oracle bones and burial rituals, and continued into the Zhou. Princely families had the right to worship their ancestors from the founder of their family line to the present. Secondary families, in theory, were only supposed to be allowed to worship their last four generations of ancestors. The head of the family acted as something like a priest of the cult and had the responsibility to see that the ancestors were properly worshipped. Powerful ancestors, like any other spirit, had to be placated and nurtured because they could still wield influence in the world and, indeed, in the affairs of the family.

This practice of worshipping one's ancestors partly explains—and in turn is explained by—the strength of the family in Chinese culture. From the earliest stages, Chinese civilization seemed to center around the family unit. The head of the family was the all but ruler of his own living family. The sense of family, though, did not include present members only, but also the dead and future generations as well. The family was viewed as an ongoing biological line, which included both past and future generations

Confucian Morality and Government

Confucius believed in government's ability to bring about not only a good society, but good individuals. Good government had the power to transform the people. A good ruler and good officials, through the power of example and through a genuine concern for the welfare of the people they governed, could, like a wind blowing over blades of grass, sway people in the direction of goodness. This is how harmony could be restored to Chinese society; this is how China could return to the Golden Age of the early Zhou period, under the glorious rules of King Wen, King Wu, and the Duke of Zhou.

To this end, the emperor himself, of course, had to be perfectly virtuous and perfectly benevolent; he had to have won the Mandate of Heaven. And, the

Emperor also had to promote good, moral men, true gentlemen, into official positions. It is these officials who could inspire the people below them into reforming themselves. Thus would a harmonious relationship between a moral emperor, moral officials, and a moral populace be established.

THE IDEOLOGICAL ASSUMPTIONS OF THE CHINESE STATE: THE ESTABLISHMENT OF A CONFUCIAN ORTHODOXY

Confucius' teachings did not become dominant overnight. Nor did everyone regard them as a solid foundation for establishing a strong, centralized government. The First emperor of the Qin dynasty, who in 221 B.C.E. had unified China under his rule and ended the period of the Warring States, embraced the teachings of Legalism instead, with their emphasis on rewards and punishments. It was his view that only strict laws and the threat of harsh punishment could result in an orderly and strong state. In 213 B.C.E., the First emperor ordered that all books that did not the serve the interests of state, including Confucian books, be turned into state authorities and burned; and that all scholars who insisted on "using the past to criticize the present," be put to death. In the following year, the First emperor executed some 460 scholars, burying them alive—or so the traditional accounts say—for defying his orders.

The Qin dynasty, though, proved to be one of the most short-lived in Chinese history. Shortly after the First emperor's death, his dynasty was overthrown and replaced by the Han dynasty. It was under the Han dynasty, in the second century B.C.E., that Confucianism became established as the dominant school of thought and the basis of Chinese imperial government. (It is important to note that for all the disesteem in which the Qin has been held by traditional Chinese historians—for its treatment of scholars and for the harshness of its laws and punishments—legalist influence in government never entirely disappeared. Chinese governments ever since saw the practical need to balance Confucian modes of governing with the application of law and punishment.)

The Han dynasty tried to establish a more bureaucratic form of central government, dividing government into three branches: 1) the military staff; 2) the civil bureaucracy; and 3) the censors whose task it was to police the officials of both the other branches. To administer these branches, the Han emperors needed a literate class they could rely upon. Convinced that individuals steeped in Confucian philosophy would be both highly literate and highly moral officials, Han emperors began recruiting their officials through a system of examinations that tested mastery of the Confucian texts. As a result, anyone who wished to have a career as a government official, the most coveted position in society, had all but to memorize the Confucian classics in the hopes of doing well on these examinations.

This system of government proved effective and continued, from the Han on, to be looked upon as the ideal form of official recruitment. Later dynasties continued and expanded the practice. Both the Tang and Song dynasties recruited their bureaucrats this way. Even the Mongol Yuan dynasty (1279-1368) concluded by the early fourteenth century that a Confucian-based examination system would produce the sorts of officials needed to govern China. After the Ming dynasty had overthrown the Mongols, it too continued the practice of recruiting its officials through this system of examinations.

Under the Ming dynasty, there were three main sets of exams. The first stage was a local certification exam given by the provincial educational commissioner. If successful, candidates received the title of "licentiate" and could now wear a distinctive cap and sash that marked their status. They were also exempted from state labor service. Often they would be recruited as private tutors for well-to-do families or as secretaries to prominent officials. To maintain their status they were required to take the exam every three years; if they failed, they would lose their licentiate status.

Having passed the first exam, licentiates were now entitled to take an exam that was offered once every three years in the provincial capital. The exam took place in three daylong sessions spread over a week. Those who passed were called "elevated men" (*juren*) and they were entitled to still more honors and privileges; and by contrast to licentiates, their status was permanent. Those who passed the provincial exam could hold lower official positions in the bureaucracy. But more importantly, having passed the provincial exam, they were entitled to compete in the metropolitan exam offered in the imperial capital a few months after the provincial exams. The metropolitan exam was part one of the third and final stage. Those who passed became "presented scholars" (*jinshi*).

After the metropolitan exam, there was still one other, mostly *pro-forma,* stage or hurdle, the palace examination, held in the presence of the emperor himself. Few failed this exam; its purpose was to determine the ranking of those who passed the metropolitan exam. The three highest ranked were appointed directly to the prestigious Hanlin Academy; from here the most capable would eventually rise into the Grand Secretariat, the body that oversaw all the branches of government. Those fortunate enough to win appointments to the Hanlin academy were publicly acclaimed, treated almost as national heroes, bringing greater fame to their families and villages. The other successful "presented scholars" would become county magistrates, provincial governors, censors, or other officials in the civil service.

Competition in the examinations was fierce. Current estimates suggest that during the Ming, probably no more than 2-5% of the candidates sitting for the licentiate degree would be successful. At the provincial examination that followed, maybe one candidate in a hundred would pass. Finally, in the metropolitan exam, perhaps 3-4% of the candidates would win the presented scholars degree. Thus, if we count only the licentiates who actually took the provincial and metropolitan examinations, about one out of every three or four thousand would have the good fortune of achieving ultimate success.

The curriculum for all of these exams was the same. It was based on what were called the Four Books. These were 1) the *Analects* of Confucius, 2) the *Book of Mencius,* a Confucian scholar from the Zhou dynasty, and two short texts, 3) the *Great Learning* and 4) the *Doctrine of the Mean.* Though the tests focused principally on the Four Books, scholars were expected to know something about the Five Classics as well. They were: 1) the *Book of Changes;* 2) the *Book of History,* a collection of sayings and speeches attributed to figures early in the Zhou dynasty; 3) *the Book of Songs,* a collection of earliest poetry; 4) *Spring and Autumn Annals,* chronicles of Zhou dynasty from 722 to

481 B.C.E. written in the state of Lu; and 5) the *Book of Rites,* collections outlining rituals and code of behavior from the early Zhou dynasty. Together the Four Books and the Five Classics constituted the core curriculum in a Confucian education; they had to be thoroughly mastered by anyone hoping to succeed in the civil service examinations.

CONCEPT OF HISTORY AND DYNASTIC RULE

The Chinese had a moral and cyclical concept of history. Each dynasty was supposed to be morally superior to the previous dynasty when it assumed power. Eventually, though, and inevitably, each dynasty would become more morally corrupt and, in time, would itself be overthrown by a new dynasty, one that was morally superior and would provide good, moral rule for the people.

According to a tradition first articulated in the early Zhou period by the Duke of Zhou, a dynasty won the right to rule from heaven. That is, because of its demonstrated virtue, heaven conferred on that dynasty the Mandate of Heaven (*tianming*). To maintain this Mandate, the dynasty and its subsequent rulers had to continue to rule wisely and virtuously, showing concern for the welfare of the people it governed. As wise and virtuous rulers were succeeded by those less wise and less virtuous, the dynasty risked losing the Mandate to a dynastic house that was more worthy. Here is how the Duke of Zhou himself explained the Mandate; speaking to the subjects of the Shang (Yin) dynasty, which the Zhou itself had just recently vanquished, he proclaimed:

Heaven has rejected and ended the Mandate of this great state of Yin. Thus, although Yin has many former wise kings in Heaven, when their successor kings and successor people undertook their Mandate, in the end wise and good men lived in misery. Knowing that they must care for and sustain their wives and children, they then called out in anguish to Heaven and fled to places where they could not be caught. Ah! Heaven too grieved for the people of all the lands, wanting, with affection, in giving its Mandate to employ those who are deeply committed. The king should have reverent care for his virtue.

Thus, a dynasty must be ever vigilant. For while it has won the Mandate of Heaven on account of its great virtue, it will readily lose that Mandate should it fail to act virtuously. The Mandate of Heaven remained the central concept in the Chinese political tradition until the twentieth century.

The rise and fall of dynasties were frequently described as morality plays in which natural disasters or invasions were attributed to the immorality of the ruling family. This was true from the first conquest of the Shang dynasty by the Zhou in 1050 B.C.E. In the *Book of History,* "The Announcement About Drunkenness" claims that the last emperors of the Shang were "addicted to drink," and thus became dissolute, neglecting altogether their paternal duties to the people. Of the final emperor, the "Announcement" says:

Greatly abandoned to extraordinary lewdness and dissipation, for pleasure's sake he ruined all his majesty. The people were all sorely grieved and wounded in heart, but he gave himself wildly up to spirits, not thinking of ceasing, but continuing his excess, till his mind was frenzied....The rank odor of the people's resentments, and the drunkenness of his herds of creatures, went loudly up on high, so that Heaven sent down ruin on Yin and showed no love for Yin—because of such excesses. There is not any cruel oppression of Heaven; people themselves accelerate their guilt, and its punishment.

Here, then, we have the Duke of Zhou claiming that the conquest of the Shang by the Zhou was mandated by Heaven on the grounds that the Shang rulers, in their dissolution, had lost all sense of moral responsibility—and thus the legitimacy to rule.

The decline of the Western Zhou dynasty (1050-770 B.C.E.) was likewise attributed to moral failure. Emperor You in the 770s became infatuated with a concubine, Baosi. To amuse her, he lit bonfires, the ordinary purpose of which was to signal distress if the capital was attacked; when the troops dutifully rushed to Emperor You's aid, only to find that in fact the capital was under no attack, Baosi smiled. Over and over he lit the beacon fires to amuse his beloved concubine. But, one day, when enemy forces actually invaded the capital and the emperor lit the bonfires to signal distress, none of his troops responded. They had tired of the game. Consequently, the capital was captured and destroyed, and Emperor You was put to death by the enemy forces. This event brought an end to the Western Zhou; and while the Zhou would move its capital eastward and continue to rule in name for another few hundred years, the rule of the so-called Eastern Zhou was mostly a fiction. The Zhou had now had but a tiny piece of territory and lost its effectiveness as a dynastic force. The moral again is clear: if Emperor You had not been distracted by his infatuation with Baosi and had attended to matters of government, carrying out his moral responsibilities to his people, he would not have lost the Mandate of Heaven.

These stories serve to illustrate how critical it was for the emperor to serve morally and conscientiously. The emperor was seen as the mediator with heaven, the figure responsible for bringing the human world (i.e., all under heaven) into full accord and harmony with the heavenly world. Sacrifices to the Altar of Heaven as well as to the imperial ancestors were intended to bring about benefits for his people, to ensure them good harvests and beneficial weather. For the emperor to lose his efficacy in communicating with heaven, or to fall from heaven's favor, would be to put the whole empire at risk. Wanli's predecessors in the Ming dynasty were well aware of this. In 1421 AD, shortly after moving the capital to Beijing, Emperor Zhu Di's new palace was struck by lightning, setting it afire. Hundreds of servants and concubines were killed. Zhu Di apparently went to the palace temple to pray, saying "The high deity is angry with me, and therefore, has burnt my palace. Although I have done no evil act; I have neither offended my father, nor mother; nor have I acted tyrannically." He admitted in a public declaration that "it seems that there has been some laxness in the rituals of honoring heaven and serving the spirits. Perhaps there has been some transgression of the ancestral rites or some perversion of government affairs? Perhaps mean men hold rank while good men flee and hide themselves, and the good and the evil are not distinguished? ... If our actions have in fact been improper, you should lay these out one by one, hiding nothing, so that we may try to reform ourselves and regain the favor of heaven."

The officials took him at his word and complained how his policies had alienated "heaven" with the heavy financial burdens he was placing on his people. He thus took immediate steps to reform the policies. This story again suggests how disasters afflicting the empire were likely to be interpreted as the consequence of the ruler's moral laxness. As the mediator between the people and heaven or nature, if he did not behave as a ruler should, he put all of his people at risk.

Oral Presentations and Writing Assignments

Requirements: **Oral participation** in class (1/3 of grade). A warning: students who have been exiled or executed cannot speak in class. Winners of the game receive an additional half grade bonus for the class participation component of the grade (B becomes B+). For the Grand Secretaries, oral participation will be of two sorts: formal presentations to the emperor, delivered from the podium; and suggestions offered in open discussion to the emperor and First Grand Secretary.

Writing: The Instructor will determine the number of required written pages for the game. Most Grand Secretaries will write two memorials. The first memorial or lecture is to be on a topic chosen by the First Grand Secretary. The second memorial is on a topic of your choice. The First Grand Secretary and Wanli emperor may choose to write whatever and whenever they wish.

Sequence of Classes

CLASS 1: INTRODUCTORY DISCUSSION OF THE ANALECTS / SELECTION OF WANLI

Students should read the game packet and the *Analects*, Books I-IX. You might want to place color-coded post-it notes or otherwise identify the particular analects that relate to IND (individual morality), RIT (ritual), ART (the arts or matters aesthetic), and GOV (matters of government).

An initial analect: Better to ponder one analect at length than to read 20 quickly.

Questions to Consider

On Good Government: As you read and reread the *Analects*, consider the following questions.

What makes for good government?

What is the relationship of the government to the people?

What are the responsibilities of the government to the people?

What are the relative roles of law and *li* (ritual, etiquette, custom) in government?

Why do people follow law? Why do people follow *li*?

How should rulers be chosen?

How does one obtain the "Mandate of Heaven"? How does one lose it?

Be prepared to discuss one analect that illuminates some of these questions.

On Being a Good Person: Consider the following questions.

What does it mean to be benevolent?

How does one pursue benevolence?

Are all people capable of benevolence?

How does a benevolent person behave toward others? What are the manifestations of a person's benevolence?

What are the rewards for being benevolent?

What is the impact of a benevolent person on others?

Be prepared to discuss one analect that illuminates some of these questions.

Reminder: The *Analects* is not a text **written** by Confucius; it is text of his teachings, as recorded and edited by disciples. The presentation thus can seem rather disjointed and aphoristic, without any apparent surface logic. But of course there is a logic to it, an underlying message. The challenge for the reader is first to make sense of each analect, then to find what gives coherence to the whole.

CLASS 2: DISCUSSION OF ANALECTS / SELECTION OF FIRST GRAND SECRETARY / DISTRIBUTION OF ROLES

Prior to class, students should have read the remainder of the *Analects*, Books X-XX, and "State and Society under the Ming" (in packet).

CLASS 3: RAY HUANG'S 1587 / FGS-WANLI INTERVIEWS / ASSIGNMENT OF 1ST MEMORIAL TOPICS

Prior to class students should have read Ray Huang, *1587: A Year of No Significance*, pp. 1-74 and "The Story of Zhang Juzheng," included in the packet.

Reading Questions for Huang's 1587

As you read Huang's *1587*, consider the following questions:

What rituals did the young Wanli emperor have to perform? Why?

When the Empress Dowager sent a letter thanking the emperor for a favor, why was it kept in the imperial archives as a state paper? (p. 5)

How was the young Wanli educated? (pp. 10-12) By whom?

Why was Tutor Chang memorialized (i.e., criticized in public memos to the emperor by lesser members of the bureaucracy)?

What were the political causes for the disgrace of Chang and Companion Feng?

Did the literary bureaucrats pervert Confucianism, or sustain it?

What was the purpose of the morning lectures by the Hanlin academicians to the Wanli emperor? Why did Shen persist in them, despite the emperor's disapproval? Why did the emperor continue to attend them?

What did Shen mean when he warned the emperor of "a cleavage between the top and the bottom" and of "a separation of the interior from the exterior"? (pp. 50-53)

Why did Tsou publicly criticize the emperor: "The best way to keep your bad deeds from the knowledge of others is not to commit them in the first place,"? (pp. 59-60)

How did Chang's drive for efficiency turn the nation against him? Was he right? (pp. 61-63)

How did Shen acquire the reputation for being a compromiser? Why did the academicians regard this as a failing?

Interviews and Memorials

Wanli and the First Grand Secretary will likely take the occasion of today's class to interview the members of the Grand Secretariat individually. Students should know their roles and be prepared on the basis of their roles to answer any questions the Emperor or FGS might pose. **NOTE: The FGS will assign first memorial topics to the Grand Secretaries.**

CLASS 4: FIRST AUDIENCE WITH WANLI; 1ST MEMORIALS

Prior to class students should finish reading Huang's *1587* (pp. 75-188) and all of the primary documents in the appendix of this book.

This session will focus on the presentation of first memorials on topics chosen by the First Grand Secretary. Grand Secretaries are encouraged to offer free commentary as they see fit; one is not obliged to be standing at the podium to offer suggestions to the emperor and the First Grand Secretary.

In preparing their first memorials, Grand Secretaries should review "State and Society under the Ming" in the appendix. This article provides general context on many of the issues the First Grand Secretary might likely assign.

A memorial written in 1517 by the great statesman and philosopher, Wang Yangming, *A Memorial on Rewards and Punishments as a Means of Encouraging the Mind-and-Hearts of the People,* is included in the appendix. Read it carefully. You are likely to find it a useful model as you prepare your own. You are free, however, to use whatever approach you think most persuasive.

(The remaining schedule will be determined by the FGS in consultation with the Gamemaster [and posted on the class website]. It may look something like what follows, depending on the number of sessions available for the game.)

CLASS 5: SECOND AUDIENCE WITH WANLI; 1ST MEMORIALS (CONT'D)

CLASS 6: THIRD AUDIENCE: EMPEROR-FGS RESPONSE / DISCUSSION

During this session, the Wanli emperor and the First Grand Secretary will respond to the first memorials. Their responses will be published. There will then be a general discussion.

CLASS 7: 2ND MEMORIALS

Each member of the Grand Secretariat must prepare a second memorial on a topic of his choice and make an oral presentation of those memorials (they should not be read, although, unlike other presentations, Grand Secretaries may read verbatim any ONE paragraph, whose wording may be crucial to the game.)

CLASS 8: 2ND MEMORIALS (CONTINUED)

CLASS 9: GAME CONCLUDES: POST MORTEM/EVALUATION

Closing Vignette: The Story of Zhang Juzheng

You push aside the nearest stack of scrolls and fumble through those at the back of your table. The copyists had spent weeks scouring the archives and gathering the materials, and you had carefully sorted them into two piles. One was the record of Zhang Juzheng (Chang Chü-cheng). He was, apart from the emperors, the most remarkable person of your lifetime—a brilliant scholar and formidable First Grand Secretary. He was also, depending on one's point of view, either a governmental reformer who saved the Ming dynasty, or a crook and a traitor who brought it to the brink of ruin. When you had requested this information about him, one of the copyists had stared at you. The past is dangerous; and you knew that those who had written about Zhang after he was gone had dealt with him harshly. To understand the man, you would have to see him through eyes untainted by his subsequent disgrace.

And you can still see him now. He was a large man, with great round shoulders that broadened into an enormous belly, his entire frame billowing out like a glorious silk tent. With his black wispy beard, long drooping moustache, and yet more facial hair along his jaw, he looked like a boulder edged in moss. Small, black eyes peered warily out from the moss.

As you prepare for tomorrow's audience with Wanli, you sense that the issues that surfaced during Zhang's tenure as First Grand Secretary are now reemerging. The new First Grand Secretary, likewise a brilliant scholar, had been a protégé of Zhang; and he speaks of the need for governmental efficiency. He even uses some of Zhang's maxims on effective laws and strict punishments.

You locate the first pile of scrolls. A document from the personnel ministry outlines the facts of Zhang's early life. He was born on May 24, 1525 in Jiangling (Huguang). Jiangling, you know, is about a week's walk west of Hankou, on the Yangzi River. Zhang's grandfather had been a palace guard for the feudal leader of the region, the prince of Liao. The next document outlines Zhang's academic record. You shake your head. In 1540, while only fifteen, he graduated as *juren*. Only seven years later, he scored highest in the regional and metropolitan exams and received his *jinshi*. He was named to the Hanlin at only twenty-two, a remarkable achievement.

Within the Forbidden City, Zhang's rare talents came to the notice of the Grand Secretariat, which assigned the young scholar the task of compiling the records for the Hanlin itself, an ideal position for learning the workings of the academy. In 1550 his wife died, and Zhang left Beijing to bury her. He returned just as a Mongol army had broached the Great Wall and placed the city under siege. Meanwhile, raiders from beyond the eastern seas were harassing villages along the southeast coast. You recall these humiliations; doubtless they were part of the reason why Zhang became a zealot in a campaign to promote government efficiency.

The next document is a copy of Zhang's request for a leave. It is dated 1554. He said he was unwell and wanted to return home. This puzzles you. Why would a man of Zhang's talents and ambition decide to abandon the seat of power? Perhaps he was frustrated by the empire's inability to crush the barbarian invaders; or perhaps he was irritated that his meteoric advance had slowed.

In any case, Zhang spent the next five years studying, traveling, and writing. You skim copies of his essays from this time. It is clear that while he was out of government, he remained preoccupied by it. In one manuscript, he called on scholars to identify more fully with the purposes of the state, and in another he proposed that they regard the teachings of the Master as an exercise in good statesmanship and not purely as matters of gentlemanly bearing and aesthetic principles.

His period of reflection ended in 1560, when he was named to serve as director of the National University; this was clearly a promotion. Three years later he edited an important publication for the Hanlin academy. Nearly everyone now remarked on his focused determination. You see a pile of papers listing Zhang's steady succession of honors and promotions: in 1566, to reader-in-waiting in charge of the Hanlin Academy; in 1567, to vice minister of Rites and chancellor of the Hanlin; and immediately thereafter to a seat on the Grand Secretariat. He advanced from grade 5A to 1B—and here the chroniclers expressed their amazement—in only two years!

In 1568 Zhang drafted his famous long memorial—you find the scroll in a separate bundle—advocating a six-point reform of the government; it systematically developed his earlier appeal for efficient government, economic growth, and development. He especially focused on addressing the plight of the peasantry and strengthening the military. The emperor—Wanli's father—apparently ignored the proposal, but it obviously impressed the scholars.

In 1571, as supervisor of the metropolitan exams, Zhang shaped the questions and model answers to ensure that new bureaucrats shared his commitment to enacting good laws and ensuring that they be obeyed. The emperor, in gratitude, conferred on him yet another honor: "Pillar of State."

The next year the emperor died, and Wanli succeeded him. The Wanli emperor was nine years old. Zhang, working adroitly with the emperor's mother, ousted the current First Grand Secretary and got himself named to the post. He now occupied a large office in the Hanlin Academy, only a few hundred steps from the emperor himself.

From this time on, Zhang personally attended to teaching the young Wanli the duties of emperor. And he could be a rather harsh taskmaster, or so it was said. He took every opportunity to lecture Wanli on the virtue of frugality, a subject that became a source of tension between them. Still, the young Wanli remained entirely dedicated to Zhang, and deferred to him on nearly everything, readily signing edicts and official documents drafted by the zealous First Grand Secretary.

And Zhang had plenty of ideas. He sought to improve the grain supply to Beijing by rebuilding much of the Grand Canal. The steady supply of grain allowed him to buy horses from the nomadic peoples to the north. Most important, Zhang tightened the screws on provincial officials. In 1573, frustrated that many refused to respond to his orders, Zhang endorsed a law obliging officials to respond to all edicts and orders in a timely fashion; those who failed to do so would be punished. Although the records show that most officials supported his measures, a handful complained that the tendency of Zhang's rulings was to increase the power of the Grand Secretariat and, by implication, the First Grand Secretary.

Official reports, written after his death, note that during these years he acquired more than power. Officials and gentry who sought his support gave him vast sums of silver; his mansion on the Yangzi reportedly cost 200,000 taels. And you recall that his robes rivaled those of the emperor.

You begin to wonder whether you, too, aspire to wear the python insignia of the First Grand Secretary and occupy an office just a few hundred steps away from that of the emperor. But you are fully aware that the job is not an easy one.

Ever since its creation in the early years of the dynasty, the position of First Grand Secretary has been fraught with difficulty. The Son of Heaven tended to view the First Grand Secretary as his spokesman and intermediary with the civil bureaucracy. From the perspective of the emperor then, the emperor issued edicts and proclamations; the First Grand Secretary elucidated them and ensured that civil officialdom at large implemented them. But over time, civil officials throughout China came to regard the position of First Grand Secretary with suspicion, even hostility. In their view, the First Grand Secretary too readily became the pawn of the emperor, or worse still, a player in the unsavory—and wholly un-Confucian—eunuch-driven factionalism at court.

Members of the Grand Secretariat themselves also voiced criticism of the First Grand Secretary. It was not the role of First Grand Secretary to acquiesce to and implement the emperor's every wish and whim; rather, as they saw it, his principal responsibility was to convince the emperor to do what they, the Grand secretaries, believed should be done. In short, a natural tension developed: the emperor believed that the First Grand Secretary worked for him, while members of the Grand Secretariat believed that the First Grand Secretary worked if not for them at least with them.

Critics of Zhang Juzheng were numerous; but they did not prevail until after he was gone. Zhang's administration during the 1570s and early 1580s was marked by success. Zhang reorganized the army and stifled resistance on the frontiers. In 1575 he focused on shaping the education of future officials. In one memorial, he indicted grade inflation and complained that graduates were often unprepared. Provincial officials were to be more diligent in teaching the texts of the Confucian Classics, and they were to pass no more than four or five candidates, not the forty or fifty as so often happened. As part of his effort to centralize standards, he cracked down on the private academies. He complained that they existed for no purpose but to help candidates pass the tests. But his critics again thought Zhang was grabbing power. The private academies, they reasoned, provided an institutional context for opposition to Zhang's regime. He closed them down to stifle dissent, or so Zhang's critics argued.

The critics had another opportunity in 1577, when Zhang's father died. By precedent and custom, Zhang should have resigned and spent the next year in mourning. But how could Zhang leave the capital then? Wanli had just turned fourteen, and, having impregnated a chambermaid, was married to her. Everyone was delighted by the possibility of a male heir, thus delivering the empire of the potential chaos of an emperor dying without a clear successor. But the young emperor needed guidance. He needed Zhang and told him so; Zhang initially demurred, citing his grief, but eventually acquiesced. He remained in Beijing, much to the dismay of the traditionalists. Zhang, they said, loved power more than his deceased father. The emperor demanded that the criticisms of Zhang cease; when several scholars persisted, he had them flogged.

In 1581, Zhang called for an empire-wide implementation of the so-called single-whip method of taxation. The single-whip system involved a number of measures, including: 1) taxation on land rather than on able-bodied males, as had been the case; 2) amalgamation of the various traditional tax and corvée items into one annual payment; 3) payment in silver rather than in kind. The system was intended both to rationalize taxation and to equalize the tax burden, that is, to ensure that all individuals, especially the wealthy landowners, were paying their fair share of taxes. It obviously was also intended to bring as much revenue as possible into the government treasury. Perhaps the most important feature of this system was a new land survey that Zhang initiated at the same time. The aim of the survey was to account for all taxable land—and to get large landholders back on to the tax registers. Needless to say, these efforts did not make Zhang a popular figure with the powerful landowning class, some of whom expressed forceful criticism of his administration. But in 1582, before the land survey could be completed, Zhang fell ill and died.

The emperor initially conferred posthumous honors on Zhang, but criticisms of the Grand Secretary resurfaced and grew ever louder. Reports of his lavish palace, and perhaps of his treason, infuriated the emperor, who cancelled the honors and dismissed many of Zhang's supporters. Eventually Wanli ordered that Zhang's sons be tortured to reveal where their father had hidden his wealth.

Governmental reformer who worked assiduously to strengthen the state and save the Ming dynasty? Or corrupt politician interested more in aggrandizing his own power and influence, a traitor who abetted the collapse of the Ming? What WAS the truth about Zhang Juzheng?

Appendix A: Primary Documents

The first two documents are from the Book of History, which, according to tradition, is a collection of speeches and proclamations of early Chinese kings and their advisers. During the Han period (206 B. C. E. - 220 A. D.), the Book of History came to be recognized as one of the Five Confucian Classics, and served until the twentieth century as a foundational text of Chinese political philosophy. No literate Chinese would be unfamiliar with the text; those who passed the civil service examination would know it by heart.

"THE CANON OF YAO" FROM THE BOOK OF HISTORY

The first document here, the "Canon of Yao," chronicles the rule of the legendary sage-ruler, Yao, said to have reigned during the 22nd century B. C. E. Most scholars now believe that this document was written quite late, indeed as late as the 2nd century B. C. E. The importance of the "Canon of Yao" lies not so much in the historical accuracy of the events that it relates, as in what it conveys of Chinese ideals of rulership. In its characterization of Yao, his government, and his selection of a successor, the reader can observe what the Chinese tradition valued in their ruler and government. The translation is from James Legge, Chinese Classics (with revision).

Examining into antiquity, we find that the Emperor Yao was called Fangxun. He was reverential, intelligent, accomplished, thoughtful, and mild. He was sincerely respectful, and capable of all complaisance. His light reached the four extremities of the empire, and extended to heaven above and earth below. Able to make bright his lofty virtue, he brought affection to the nine classes of his kindred. When the nine branches of his kindred had all become harmonious, he regulated and polished the hundred clans. When the hundred clans had all become illustrious, he harmonized the myriad states of the empire. Lo! The black-haired people were transformed. The result was universal concord.

Thereupon Yao commanded Xi and He, in reverent accordance with their observation of the wide heavens, to calculate and delineate the movements and appearances of the sun, the moon, the stars, and the zodiacal spaces; and so to deliver respectfully the seasons to the people....

The emperor said, "Ah! You, Xi and He, a round year consists of three hundred, sixty, and six days. By means of an intercalary month do you fix the four seasons, and complete the determination of the year. Thereafter, if you sincerely regulate the various officers, all the works of the year will be fully performed."

The emperor said, "Who will search out for me a man according to the times, whom I may raise and employ?" Fang Qi said, "There is your heir-son Zhu, who is highly intelligent." The emperor said, "Alas! He is insincere and quarrelsome: how can he do?"

The emperor said, "Who will search out for me a man equal to the exigency of my affairs?" Huan Dou said, "Oh! There is the Minister of Works, whose merits have just been displayed in various ways." The emperor said, "Alas! When unemployed, he can talk; but when employed, his actions turn out differently. He is respectful only in appearance. See! The floods assail the heavens."

The emperor said, "Oh! Chief of the Four Mountains, destructive in their overflow are the waters of the inundation. In their vast extent they embrace the mountains and overtop the hills, threatening the heavens with their floods, so that the lower people groan and murmur. Is there a capable man, to whom I can assign the correction of this calamity? All in the court said, "Oh! There is Gun. "The emperor said, "Alas! No, by no means! He is disobedient to orders, and injures his kin." The Chief of the Four Mountains said, "Well but---. Try him, and then you can have done with him." The emperor said to Gun, "Go; and be reverent!" For nine years he labored, but the work was unaccomplished.

The emperor said, "Oh! You Chief of the Four Mountains, I have been on the throne for seventy years. You can carry out my appointments;--I will resign my throne to you." The Chief of the Four Mountains said, "I have not the virtue; I should only disgrace the imperial seat." The emperor said, "Point out some one among the illustrious, or set forth one from among the poor and mean." All in the court said to the emperor, "There is an unmarried man among the lower people, called Shun of Yu." The emperor said, "Yes, I have heard of him. What is his character?" The Chief of the Four Mountains said, "He is the son of a blind man. His father was obstinately unprincipled; his step-mother was insincere; his half brother Xiang was arrogant. He has been able, however, by his filial piety to live in harmony with them, and to lead them gradually to self-government, so that they no longer proceed to great wickedness." The emperor said, "I will try him! I will wive him, and then see his behavior with my two daughters." On this he gave orders, and sent down his two daughters to the north of the Gui River, to be wives in the family of Yu. The emperor said, "Be reverent!"

"THE SHAO ANNOUNCEMENT" FROM THE BOOK OF HISTORY

This second document, the "Shao Announcement," is a proclamation made by either the Duke of Shao or the Duke of Zhou (modern scholars disagree) to the people of the Shang (i.e., Yin) just after the Zhou conquest of the Shang. (We take it here to be delivered by the Duke of Zhou.) The Duke attempts to explain the reason for the Zhou action against the Shang and its final success. It is a powerful piece of political rhetoric, even propaganda, attempting to justify the Shang defeat in terms of an entirely new political concept, the Mandate of Heaven.

This document, likely from the 11ᵗʰ century B. C. E., presents the earliest articulation of the concept of the Mandate of Heaven, a concept that would remain at the very center of Chinese political ideology until modern times. The translation is from James Legge, Chinese Classics (with revision).

Oh! August heaven, Shangdi, has changed his mandate in favor of his eldest son, and this great dynasty of Yin (i.e., Shang). Our king has received that mandate. Unbounded is the happiness connected with it, and unbounded is the anxiety. Oh, how can he be other than reverent?

When heaven rejected and made an end of the mandate in favor of the great state of Yin, there were many of the former intelligent kings of Yin in heaven. The king, however, who had succeeded to them, the last of their race, from the time of his entering into their appointment, proceeded in such a way as at last to keep the wise in obscurity and the vicious in office. The poor people in such a case, carrying their children and leading their wives, made their moan to heaven. They even fled away, but were apprehended again. Oh, heaven had compassion on the people of the four quarters; its favoring mandate lighted on our earliest founders. Let the king sedulously cultivate the virtue of reverence.

Look at the former peoples of ancient times, the Xia. Heaven guided, nourished, and protected them; they strove to understand what heaven favored. But these days they have lost their mandate. Now look at the Yin. Heaven guided, regulated, and protected them; they strove to understand what heaven favored. But these days they have lost their mandate.

Now our young king has succeeded to the throne—let him not slight the aged and the experienced, for it may be said of them that they have studied the virtuous conduct of our ancient worthies, and still more, that they have matured their plans in the light of heaven.

Oh, although the king is young, yet he is the eldest son of heaven. Let him but effect a great harmony with the people. With the present blessing (from heaven), let the king dare not be remiss; he should be apprehensive about the dangers that the people pose.

May the king come and carry on for Shangdi; let him personally undertake the duties of government in the center of the land. I, Dan (Duke of Zhou), say, 'Now that this great city has been built, may he from this place be the counterpart to august heaven, taking great care to sacrifice to spirits above and below. From this place may he centrally govern.' If the king possesses the mandate in perfection, the government of the people will enjoy the blessings (of heaven).

Let the king first bring under his influence the Yin managers of affairs, associating them with our Zhou managers of affairs so as regulate their natures, and they will make daily progress.

Let the king be reverent in practicing that virtue that requires reverence. We cannot but mirror ourselves in the Xia; at the same time, we cannot but mirror ourselves in the Yin. We do not presume to know and say, 'the Xia was to enjoy the mandate of heaven for so-and-so many years'; nor do we presume to know and say, 'it could not continue longer.' The fact was simply that, for want of reverent attention to their virtue, they lost their mandate early. Now the king has succeeded them in receiving their mandate. We should reflect on the mandates of these two states, and succeed them with similar achievements. The king now begins to undertake the mandate....

It is for him who is in the position of king to overtop all with his virtue. In this case the people will imitate him throughout the whole empire, and the king will become more illustrious.

May those above and below labor with a common anxiety, saying, 'As we receive the mandate of heaven, let it greatly be like the Xia's long-continued years and not fail of the Yin's long-continued years.' We wish the king, through the small people, to receive a long-abiding mandate from heaven.

EXCERPT FROM DISCOURSES ON SALT AND IRON

In 81 B. C. E. the emperor issued an order to senior officials of government and wise men of the empire to come together in an attempt to reach an understanding of the hardships faced by the population of the time. A record of this conference was kept, resulting in the Discourses on Salt and Iron (the title is taken after the topic raised first at the conference). The deliberations, as recorded in this document, were wide-ranging, touching on most of the major intellectual, political, and economic issues of the day. At the center of all these issues was the role of imperial government: its aims, duties, and responsibilities. Administrative spokesmen argued that the role of government is to provide for the material needs of the people and to ensure their safety against nomadic invasion, especially by the Xiongnu tribes to the north. The wise men, or literati, countered that government should be less invested in matters that would bring profit to the treasury—and incidentally to government officials—and more interested in establishing a cultured, fully moral society based on agrarian principles, through the leadership and example provided by moral government. The Discourses, though written in the Han, achieved great prominence and was well-known to literate Chinese throughout imperial times, especially those in government circles. It is especially interesting to us because it deals with similar issues to those confronting the Ming: how best to raise government revenue; the legitimacy of government monopolies; how to deal effectively with the threat of "barbarians"; the relative weight to be given to the power of moral leadership, on the one hand, and the efficacy of strong governmental action and policy, on the other. The following is excerpted from chapter one of the text. The translation is from Esson Gale, Discourses on Salt and Iron (E. J. Brill, 1931), with revision.

It so happened that in the sixth year of the shiyuan era [81 B. C. E.] an Imperial edict directed the Chancellor and the Imperial secretaries to confer with the recommended Worthies and Literati, and to enquire of them as to the rankling grievances among the people.

The Literati responded as follows: It is our humble opinion that the principle of ruling men lies in nipping in-the bud wantonness and frivolity, in extending wide the elementals of virtue, in discouraging secondary occupations, and in displaying benevolence and righteousness. Let lucre never be paraded before the eyes of the people; only then will moral instruction flourish and the customs of the people improve. But now, with the system of the salt and iron monopolies, the liquor excise, and equable marketing, established in the provinces, the Government has entered into competition with the people for profit, dispelling rustic generosity and sanctioning greed. As a result few among our people take up the primary occupations [farming], while many flock to the secondary ones [trade]. As artifice thrives, basic simplicity declines; as secondary occupations flourish, the primary ones suffer. When the secondary is cultivated, the people become decadent; but when primary is cultivated, the people become simple and sincere. The people being sincere, wealth will abound; but when the people are extravagant, cold and hunger will follow. We recommend that the salt, iron and liquor monopolies and the system of equable marketing be abolished so that the primary pursuits may be advanced, and the secondary ones expelled. This will have the advantage of increasing the profits from agriculture.

The Lord Grand Secretary [Sang Hongyang] said: The Xiongnu [the "barbarians" to the north] have rebelled against our authority and frequently raided and devastated the frontier settlements. If we properly prepare for them we place a great strain upon the soldiery of the Middle Kingdom;

but if we do not, their incursions will never cease. The late Emperor [Wu, r. 141-87 B.C.E.] pitied the border people who for so long had suffered distress and hardship and been carried off as prisoners. Therefore, he built defense stations, made ready a system of warning beacons, and set up garrisons to protect the border areas. When the revenue for the defense of the frontier fell short, the salt and iron monopoly was established, and the liquor excise and the system of equable marketing introduced; funds were raised to furnish border expenditures. Now our critics here, who demand that these measures be abolished, at home would have the hoard of the treasury entirely depleted, and abroad would deprive the border of provision for its defense; they would expose our soldiers who defend the passes and patrol the walls to all the hunger and cold of the borderland. How else can we provide for them? It is not expedient to abolish these measures!

The Literati: Confucius observed that the head of a state or a noble family worries not about underpopulation but about uneven distribution, not about poverty but about instability (Analects 16.1). Thus the Son of Heaven should not speak about much and little, the feudal lords should not talk about advantage and detriment, ministers about gain and loss, but they should cultivate benevolence and righteousness, to set an example to the people, and extend wide their virtuous conduct to gain the people's confidence. Then will nearby folk lovingly flock to them and distant peoples joyfully submit to their authority. Therefore the master conqueror does not fight; the expert warrior needs no soldiers; the truly great commander requires not to set his troops in battle array. Cultivate virtue in the temple and the hall, then you need only to show a bold front to the enemy and your troops will return home in victory. The Prince who practices benevolent administration should be matchless in the world; for him, what use is expenditure?

The Lord Grand Secretary: The Xiongnu, savage and wily, boldly push through the passes and harass the Middle Kingdom, massacring the provincial population and killing the keepers of the Northern Marches. They long deserve punishment for their unruliness and lawlessness. But Your Majesty graciously took pity on the insufficiency of the multitude and did not suffer his lords and knights to be exposed in the desert plains, yet unflinchingly. You cherish the purpose of raising strong armies and driving the Xiongnu before You to their original haunts in the north. I again assert that the proposal to do away with the salt and iron monopoly and equable marketing would grievously diminish our border supplies and impair our military plans. I can not consider favorably a proposal so heartlessly dismissing the border question.

The Literati: The ancients held in honor virtuous methods and discredited resort to arms. Thus Confucius said: If distant subjects are unsubmissive, one cultivates one's moral quality in order to attract them, and once they have come one makes them content (Analects 16.1) Now these virtuous principles are discarded and reliance put on military force; troops are raised to attack the enemy and garrisons are stationed to make ready for him. It is the long drawn-out service of our troops in the field and the ceaseless transportation of necessary food supplies that cause our soldiers on the marches to suffer from hunger and cold abroad, while the common people are burdened with labor at home. The establishment of the salt and iron monopoly and the institution of finance officials to supply the army needs were not permanent schemes; it is therefore desirable that they now be abolished.

The Lord Grand Secretary: In antiquity, the founders of our state made open the ways for both primary and secondary occupations facilitated equitable distribution of goods. Markets and courts were provided to harmonize various demands; there people of all classes gathered together and all goods collected, so that farmer, merchant, artisan and teacher could each obtain what he desired; the exchange completed, everyone went back to his occupation. Facilitate exchange so that the people will be unflagging, says the Book of Changes. Thus without artisans, the farmers will be deprived of the use of implements; without merchants, all prized commodities will be cut off. The former would lead to stoppage of grain production, the latter to exhaustion of wealth. It is clear that the salt and iron monopoly and equable marketing are really intended for the circulation of amassed wealth and the regulation of the consumption according to the urgency of the need. It is inexpedient to abolish them.

The Literati: Lead the people with virtue and the people will return to generosity; entice the people with gain and they will become heartless. Being heartless they will turn their backs on righteousness to pursue profit; pursuing profit people will swarm the roads and throng the marketplaces. A poor country may appear plentiful, not because it possesses abundant wealth, but because wants multiply and people become reckless, said Laozi. Hence the true King promotes primary pursuits and discourages secondary ones…Consequently, merchants are for the purpose of trading goods that are plentiful but not circulating widely, and artisans are for the purpose of providing tools. These are not central concerns of government.

The Lord Grand Secretary:…The scarlet lacquer and pennant feathers of Long and Shu, the leather goods, bone and ivory of Jing and Yang, the cedars, lindera, and bamboo rods of Jiangnan, the fish, salt, rugs, and furs of Yan and Qi, the lustrous yarn, linen, and hemp-cloth of Yan and Yu, are all necessary commodities to maintain our lives and provide for our death. But we depend upon the merchants for their distribution and on the artisans for giving them their finished forms. This is why the Sages availed them of boats and bridges to negotiate rivers and galleys, and domesticated cattle and horses for travel over mountains and plateaus. Thus by penetrating to distant lands and exploring remote places, they were able to exchange all goods to the benefit of the people. Hence His late Majesty [Emperor Wu] established officers in control of iron to meet the farmer's needs and provided equable marketing to make sufficient the people's wealth. Thus, the salt and iron monopoly and the equable marketing supported by the myriad people and looked to as the source of supply, cannot conveniently be abolished.

The Literati: That a country possesses a wealth of fertile land and yet its people are underfed is due to the fact that merchants and artisans have prospered unduly while the primary occupations have been neglected. That a country possesses rich natural resources in its mountains and seas and yet its people lack wealth is because the people's necessities have not been attended to, while luxuries and fancy articles have multiplied….

The Lord Grand Secretary: Formerly the princes in the provinces sent in their respective products as tribute, but the transportation was confusing and troublesome; and the goods were usually of such distressingly bad quality that they were not worth the cost of transportation. Therefore transportation offices have been provided in every province to assist in the delivery and shipping and for speeding tribute from outlying areas. So the system came to be known as equable marketing. Warehouses have been established in the capital for the storing of goods buying when prices are low and selling when prices are high, with the result that the government suffers no loss and the merchants cannot speculate for profit. This is therefore known as the balancing standard. With the balancing standard people are safeguarded from unemployment; with the equable marketing the burden of labor service is made equal. Thus, the balancing standard and equable marketing are measures designed to equalize the myriad goods and to benefit the people, not to open the way to profit and serve as a ladder of crime for the people.

The Literati: The ancients, in levying and taxing the people, took from them what they were skilled at, and did not demand from them what they were poor at. Thus the farmers contributed the fruits of their labor, the weaving women, their products. Now the government leaves alone what the people have and exacts from them what they have not, so that they are forced to sell their products at a cheap price to satisfy demands from above…. The farmers suffer twice over while the weaving women are doubly taxed. We have not yet seen that your marketing is "equable". The government officers swarm about, closing doors, gaining control of the market, and cornering all the goods. With the goods cornered, prices soar; with prices soaring, the merchants reap profits from their own dealings. The officials are lenient with unscrupulous bullies, and the merchants store up goods and accumulate commodities waiting for a time of need. Slick traders and unscrupulous officials buy in cheap to get high returns. We have not yet seen that your standard is "balanced". For it seems that in ancient times equable marketing was to bring about equitable division of labor and facilitate transportation of tribute; it was surely not for profit or to make trade in commodities.

Confucianism and the Succession Crisis of the Wanli Emperor

A MEMORIAL ON REWARDS AND PUNISHMENTS AS A MEANS OF ENCOURAGING THE MIND-AND-HEARTS OF THE PEOPLE (SUBMITTED IN THE TWELFTH YEAR OF THE ZHENGDE REIGN [1517])

Wang Yangming (1472-1529) was one of the most renowned Confucian thinkers and statesmen of the Ming dynasty. In 1499, he received the jinshi degree, and thereafter served in a number of important official positions. In 1516 he was appointed governor of southern Jiangxi province, an area of mountains and forests, an ideal lair for robbers and bandit gangs. The following memorial submitted by Wang in 1517 to the Zhengde emperor shows the determination with which Wang tackled what had become a banditry crisis. In it, he lays out what he believes to be the reasons for the crisis, and then suggests measures the government, namely the emperor, ought to take to bring the crisis under control.

Wang's memorial illustrates the way in which Chinese officials—of all ranks—would typically invoke the wisdom and lessons from the past to solve the political and administrative problems of the present. In preparing their own memorials to the Wanli emperor, students should do likewise.

I have received and respectfully considered the petition from Vice Commissioner for Provincial Surveillance and Military Defense of Lingbei Circuit of Jiangxi Province, Yang Cheng….

He goes on for a few paragraphs to describe in general terms what he has learned about the conditions of banditry in the area under his jurisdiction. Then he turns to the more detailed analysis that follows.

Bandits by nature are normally ferocious and obstinate, and yet they remain fearful of chastisement. It is only when they escape chastisement for their acts of banditry, and, further, are pardoned and invited to surrender, that they become reckless and show no fear of the authorities.

Take the bandits in Southern Jiangxi: the common people who had suffered at their hands would, at first, join together to oppose them, or they would complain to the officials for redress, relying on the power of the authorities to uphold law and order. But the authorities, considering that the bandits would be invited to surrender in any case, did not bother to take up such cases for them. The bandits, on their part, well knowing that the authorities would not interfere with them, would further oppress the people and harass them even to a greater extent. The people, finding such a situation intolerable and the authorities not to be depended on, would take the natural course of joining banditry. As a result, the bandits, feeling reassured, would come out to rob and plunder even more frequently than before, as they knew that the authorities would sooner or later offer to pacify them. The people, being devoid of any support, would turn themselves into bandits in greater number, as they knew that the authorities could not give them any assistance. When the good people could find no relief from wrong or oppression, the bandits could have all that they wanted; when the common people were groaning under heavy taxation, the bandits were often bestowed with rewards and bounties. Indeed why should they not cast their lot with the bandits? Therefore, those who live close to the bandits would defend or fight for them; those who live far from the bandits would serve them as their guides; those who live in towns or the suburbs would have intercourse with them, and those who work in the government offices would act as their spies. At first they did so simply with the idea of avoiding trouble, but later, they acted for the sake of gain. Hence there is the thesis that prevalence of banditry is due to indiscriminate pacification.

The evil of banditry has tried the temper of gods and induced the resentment of men. Who would not feel deeply afflicted by it? And yet the authorities insist upon pacifying the bandits, because they are compelled to do so by circumstances. Should the soldiers be strong and daring enough to kill bandit leaders or to demolish bandit dens, then, at one stroke, they might redress the grievances of the people, rid a locality of its menace and achieve merits and distinction. Would not that be their very ambition? Soldiers in Southern Jiangxi, however, are not trained, and are generally weak, haughty and indolent. When they are ordered to the front, they resist summonses and even arrests and can not be assembled within less than ten days. After they are duly organized and dispatched on their way, it takes them another ten days to reach their destination. By that time the bandits have gathered their spoils and returned back to their nests. Perchance, the bandits might not have retired, these soldiers would flee for their lives at sight of the dust [raised by the bandits] or would disperse without any actual fighting. With such troops to withstand the bandits, it might be likened to setting a drove of sheep to attack a group of tigers. How can there be any other recourse but to invite the bandits to surrender?…

Good leaders in ancient times were able to muster a crowd of the market to go to battle or to rally dispersed soldiers to oppose a strong savage force. Now there still are several thousand soldiers in Southern Jiangxi. Can it be the case that none of them is serviceable? And yet, they would not halt at the sound of the gong, nor would they charge forward at the sound of the drum. They would flee before gaining a view of the enemy, and would be defeated without any actual conflict. Why? Because if they risk their lives in pushing forward, there is not the inducement of any reward, or ennoblement, and if they retreat or make their escape, neither is there any death penalty. On the contrary, there would be certain death in advancing, while they may yet live in retreating. Why should they then seek certain death? Wu Qi (4th c. B.C.E. expert in the art of warfare) once said: "If laws and orders be not clear, if rewards and punishments be not just, though there be a hundred thousand men at arms, they are of no avail." It is the nature of militia that when they fear their own leader, they are not afraid of the enemy; and that when they fear the enemy, they are not afraid of their own leader. Now the soldiers in Southern Jiangxi are usually afraid of the bandits and do not fear their own leader. It would be futile to expect them to be of any use. Therefore it is maintained that the inefficiency of the armed forces is due to the unenforcement of rewards and punishments.

Now the Imperial Court has already established rules for the awarding of rewards and the inflicting of punishments, but has not yet made them perfectly clear to the populace nor has carried them out. In ancient times, rewards were not bestowed delinquently, nor were punishments meted out after the lapsing of the causes. For, to give rewards delinquently, it would be equal to no rewards being bestowed at all, and to mete out punishments after the lapsing of the causes, it would be equivalent to inflicting no punishments at all. If no rewards were conferred even after the passing of the time, or no punishments were dealt out even after the lapsing of the causes, how could we unite the soldiers as of one mind, or rouse their spirits? Under such circumstances, even with [the legendary generals] Han and Bai as generals, such an attempt might not be successful. What then could be expected of a literary dolt who is limited in his knowledge and experience and is ignorant of military affairs like Your minister?…

Your minister has recently selected from the troops in Southern Jiangxi over two thousand men who are endowed with the best fighting qualities and has organized them by means of strict discipline and constant training. They are now passable. If the rules for reward and punishment that are in force with the grand army engaged in punitive expeditions are to be applied to troops

Confucianism and the Succession Crisis of the Wanli Emperor

engaged in bandit suppression in time of peace, and if Your minister be granted discretionary power without any restriction as to time but under the sole responsibility of achieving successes, then in comparison with the dispatching of large armies, Your minister would be able to perform twice the amount of meritorious services at half the amount of expenses....

It is, therefore, earnestly hoped that Your Majesty will, in consideration of the increasing rampancy of banditry, in compassion of the gradual augmentation of the people's depression, in grieving over the intensification of the calamities suffered by the localities and in commiseration of the unredressibility of the grievances of the people, specially order the Board of War that the present proposal might be accepted and grant Your minister authority-banners and authority-tablets [i.e., tokens of imperial authority used by field commanders] so that Your minister may exercise his functions under such authority. In the event of there being troops lacking in training, or banditry at large, Your ministers will not be able to escape from the death penalty. It was on account of the responsibility not being exclusive, the authority not being great, and rules for rewards and punishments not being enforced, that the army had been ineffective and bandit suppression become a failure. It was after such experience that a high official has been selected and given the power of a general commander to retrieve the situation. Even if good arrangements could be made for the future, what had been lost before was not recoverable.

As Your minister is limited in knowledge, lacking in experience, and, at the same time, weak in body and ill in health, he is conscious that he is not up to the task expected of him. He will soon ask Your Majesty's leave to vacate his post and to breathe his last in the woods. However, as he is still in his office, he dares not refrain from unburthening his mind before Your Imperial Majesty on what he knows to be an evil. If Your Majesty will grant his request, so that his successor may reap the benefit to some extent and achieve successes in suppressing the bandits, Your minister may thereby lessen the enormity of his guilt.

To explain the use of rewards and punishments as a means of encouraging the mind-and-hearts of the people, I have drawn up this document. I ask for Your Majesty's instruction.

(Translation from Chang Yü-chüan, *Wang Shou-jen as a Statesman* [University Publications of America, rpt., 1975], with minor revision.)

Appendix B: "State and Society under the Ming"

From *China: Tradition and Transformation*, edited by John K. Fairbank and Edwin O. Reischauer (Houghton Mifflin: Boston 1989) "State and Society under the Ming" (Ch. 8, pp. 177-210)

CHINESE "CULTURALISM"

The Ming period from 1368 to 1644 is one of the great eras of orderly government and social stability in human history. A population averaging around 100 million lived during 276 years in comparative peace. The sub-sequent change from Ming to Ch'ing rule was relatively easy. The decline of Ming power and the Manchu capture of Peking in 1644 were followed by the Manchu conquest of all China. But this warfare and its devastation seem limited in comparison with the organized looting and massacres of contemporary European armies during the Thirty Years' War of 1648. In any case, so stable was the political and social order of the Ming that it persisted, basically unaltered, under the alien Ch'ing dynasty for another 267 years from 1644 to 1912. Thus from the middle of the fourteenth century to the beginning of the twentieth, China followed traditional ways.

Unfortunately for the Chinese people of recent times, this remarkable stability was maintained during those very centuries that saw the dynamic rise of modern Europe
the Renaissance, the Reformation, the growth of national states, their expansion into the New World and over the earth, followed by the French Revolution and the Industrial Revolution. None of these fundamental Western transformations of the last six centuries had a real counterpart in China's own experience. China remained outside the turbulent stream of Western history, which was moving to engulf the world, and consequently by the nineteenth century had fallen behind the West in many aspects of material culture and technology as well as in economic and political organization. This long period of stability in East Asian civilization left it comparatively "backward" or "underdeveloped." But this comparison with the expanding West should not stigmatize the Ming and Ch'ing periods as retrogressive or overshadow their real achievements, As we learn more about these centuries, we may expect to find many evidences of innovation and growth. Chinese society was far from unchanging, but the pace was slower and the degree of change less than in the West.

One factor creating stability was the Chinese view of history as "change within tradition." The leaders of society were devoted to tradition; any-thing that happened in the present had to be fitted into the rich pattern of experience inherited from the past. Instead of the ideal of progress, which Westerners today have inherited from the nineteenth century, the Chinese of the Ming and saw their ideal models far in the past.

This turning back for inspiration to the great ages of Han, T'ang, and Sung was accompanied by a deep resentment against the Mongols. Alien rule had inspired hostility toward alien things in general. Gradually this view hardened into a lack of interest in anything beyond the pale of Chinese civilization. This turning away from the outside world was ac-companied by a growing introspection within Chinese life. We have al-ready seen this in the antiquarian interest in art and in the burst of historical scholarship in the Sung. From that time on a degree of mingled fear and contempt for the outside world and a narrow concentration on the exclusively Chinese way of life produced a growing ethnocentrism. Eventually it dominated China's foreign relations and gave her an intellectual and psychological immunity to foreign stimuli.

This attitude had much in common with modern nationalism. But there were differences. A nationalist group asserts its own distinctiveness and superiority because it fears not only political but also cultural inundation by some other group. Nationalism thus seems closely tied to a general feeling of competition and insecurity. It is commonly asserted by a cultural subunit, particularly a linguistic subgroup, against other subunits within the same culture, as in the rise of national states within the common culture of Western Christendom. The Chinese, by contrast, showed no sign of a feeling of cultural inferiority. Political subjugation may have been feared, but cultural conquest was unimaginable. Thus Chinese xenophobia was combined with a complete confidence in cultural superiority. China reacted not as a cultural subunit, but as a large ethnocentric universe which remained quite sure of its cultural superiority even when relatively inferior in military power to fringe elements of its universe. Because of these similarities to and differences from nationalism, we call this earlier Chinese attitude "culturalism," to suggest that in the Chinese view the significant unit was really the whole civilization rather than the narrower political unit of a nation within a larger cultural whole.

Underlying this devotion to the Chinese way of life was one primary political fact, that the whole Middle Kingdom remained an administrative unit under a central government. This remarkable cohesiveness, compared with the constant disunity among the relatively smaller European states, cannot be attributed to geography. It normally took a month or so for the emperor's writ to be carried by horse to the borders of the realm in Kwangtung, Yunnan, Central Asia, or the Northeast, farther than any distances in Western Europe. China's inveterate unity must be explained on institutional grounds, by the habits of thought and action that had become established in the society. The Chinese state was regarded as coterminous with Chinese culture. There was such a close identification of the entire way of life with the unified empire that the one implied the other. It was as if the Roman Empire had persisted in the West and had prevented the rise of France, England, and the other nations. The identity of culture and polity made the Chinese leadership of the Ming and Ch'ing periods uninterested in, and at times hostile to, things foreign. Culturalism thus was a pervasive attitude throughout the period.

GOVERNMENT UNDER THE MING

The Founding of the Ming Dynasty.   The weakening of Mongol rule was hastened by fratricidal rivalry within the imperial clan. Fifteen years of frequent famine in North China after 1333 were capped by severe floods of the Yellow River. Flood and famine depleted the granaries. During the 1340's, uprisings occurred sporadically in nearly every province. In 1351–1353 several major rebel leaders emerged, and a typical interdynastic contest began among them to determine who should survive as the fittest to inherit the Mandate of Heaven. Some of these men claimed descent from the Sung emperors, some invoked a religious sanction by prophesying the advent of the Bodhisattva Maitreya, the Buddha of the Future, and others had the help of secret societies. The most famous of all secret societies has been the White Lotus Society. Its origin as a sect of T'ien-t'ai Bud-dhism has been traced back directly to the first half of the twelfth century. As with any group that opposed the ruling dynasty, this society had to be secret in order to survive.

The eventual winner among all these Chinese rebel heroes was Chu Yüan-chang (1328–1398) whose name ranks with that of Liu Pang, the founder of the Han, as a humble commoner who through native ability in a time of opportunity became the Son of Heaven. He was born in the Huai River region northwest of Nanking. Left an orphan, he entered a Buddhist monastery as a novice, which gave him a chance to become literate. For a time he even begged for a living. But in 1352, at the age of twenty-five, he joined a rebel band. (Probably he also joined the White Lotus Society, but he later denied this-it was an unwise precedent to leave in the historical record.)

Chu and his band crossed the Yangtze and in 1356 seized Nanking, a strategic base close to the key economic area of the Yangtze delta. By 1367, after defeating rival regimes both upstream and downstream, he controlled all the Yangtze Valley. Meanwhile, the Mongol commanders, instead of attacking the Chinese rebels, fought among themselves. In 1368 Chu Yüan-chang seized Peking but continued to use Nanking as his capital. He proclaimed himself the first emperor of the Ming ("Brilliant") dynasty, and chose Hung-wu ("Vast military power") as the name of the "year period," but, by keeping it for his whole reign, the first Ming emperor transformed it into his reign title. This set a fashion throughout the Ming and Ch'ing, of using only one year-period name during a whole reign, so that emperors of this era are generally known by their reign titles.

A second strong ruler was Yung-lo (reigned 1403–1424). The fourth son of Hung-wu, he had his base of power in Peking, where he rebelled against his nephew, Hung-wu's grandson, who had inherited the throne at Nanking. He waged a devastating civil war until he finally captured Nanking, and as a usurper at the age of forty-three took as his reign title Yung-lo ("Perpetual Happiness").

Nanking had been built up by Hung-wu as the imperial capital, with a city wall sixty feet high and over twenty miles around, the longest city wall in the world. Yung-lo in 1421 moved the Ming capital to Peking, leaving Nanking as the subsidiary capital. He rebuilt Peking on a more extensive plan than that of the Mongols. The main city walls, forty feet high and more than fourteen miles around, formed a square with nine gates, each one protected by an outer gate. In the center stood the walls of the Imperial City, some five miles in perimeter. Within it, in turn, were the high red walls of the Forbidden City, the imperial palace itself, surrounded by a moat about two miles around. Running from south to north through the palace, on the main axis of the whole capital, are the imposing throne halls with their gold-tiled roofs, each one rising from a terrace of white marble. Much of this great architectural creation of the Ming still stands today as an unparalleled monument of empire. The walls of the southern city of Peking with their seven additional gates were added in the sixteenth century.

Ming Despotism. The seventeen Ming emperors reigned during a series of recognizable phases: (1) the inaugural era of founding and consolidation under Hung-wu (1368–1398); (2) the vigorous building and expansion under Yung-lo (1403–1424) and his successors,

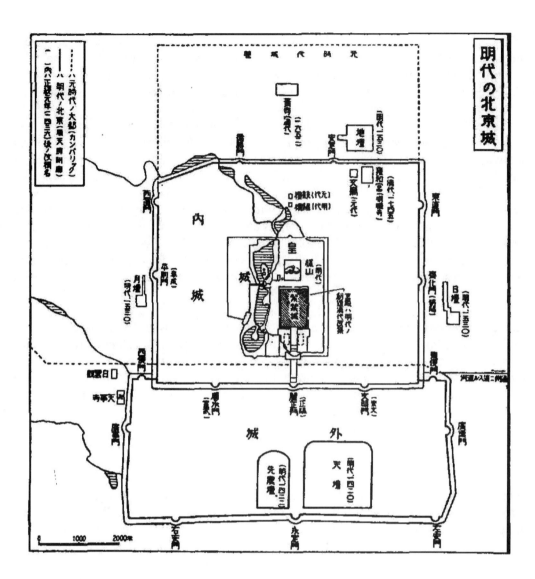

PEKING UNDER THE MING AND CH'ING. *Top and center: Site of Yüan Capital, Tai-tu, of which the northern walls were razed by the Ming. Center: Inner City surrounds Imperial City which encloses lakes on left and Forbidden City or Palace on main axis, with Prospect Hill (dredged from lakes) on north. Bottom: Outer city (under the Manchus, the "Chinese City") with Altars of Heaven (right) and of Agriculture (left). Outside the main city on east, north, and west, respectively, are Altars of the Sun, Earth, and Moon. (From Wada Sei,* Tōyō bunkashi taikei.)*

which, however, by the middle of the century had overstrained the imperial resources; (3) a century of gradual decline of imperial power both at home and abroad; (4) in the latter part of the sixteenth century a period of reform; and (5) by the early seventeenth century an intensification of evils and final collapse.

This profile was studied intensively by moralistic Confucian scholars in the late Ming, who saw the Chinese state collapsing. They and their successors in the Ch'ing made a moral interpretation of the dynastic decline, analyzing the personal failings of successive emperors, the errors of their officials, and the factionalism which rent the bureaucracy. Today, our basic political criticism might be that the emperor was subject to no higher law or constitutional checks. Power was concentrated in him personally. He had to be either a benevolent despot or tyrant, or else let his power be exercised by others as favorites on an irregular, unstable, personal basis. The Ming government had to have a great man at its head or face disaster.

Because the founder of the Ming, ruling for thirty-two years, left his imprint so strongly upon the dynasty, his personality was of special significance. Hung-wu was represented in his portraits as a man with an ugly, porcine face. He had had a hard life in his youth, and as emperor remained lonely and austere. He made a fetish of frugality and became subject to fears and suspicions, sometimes to delusions and violent out-bursts of temper. He became very cruel and inflicted terrible tortures for slight offenses. In his final will he wrote: "For thirty-one years I have labored to discharge Heaven's will, tormented by worries and fears, without relaxing for a day." Perhaps this rather paranoid temperament of the founder helps to explain the growth of the Ming despotism. Hung-wu's concentration of power in his own hands may also have derived from his experience as a self-made conqueror of pre-eminent capacity. He institutionalized his personal role.

In 1380, suppressing a widespread plot attributed to his chief minister, Hung-wu abolished the central administrative organ of past dynasties, the Imperial Secretariat. Henceforth the emperor's rule was to be personal and direct. This institutional change gave the emperors of the Ming and also the Ch'ing periods a more autocratic role. In his personal administration Hung-wu, however, made use of Grand Secretaries, who handled the flow of official memorials (as many as a hundred a day) and drafted the imperial edicts in reply. Eventually they became institutionalized informally as the Grand Secretariat, a sort of cabinet, superior to the Six Ministries. But the Grand Secretaries remained merely aides of the ruler, unable to take executive action on their own initiative.

One group who eventually acquired considerable power were the eunuchs. Hung-wu had warned vigorously against this very possibility. He erected in the palace a metal tablet three feet high reading, "Eunuchs must have nothing to do with administration." He limited their numbers, ranks, titles, and style of clothing, forbade their handling documents, dismissed those who commented on government affairs, and decreed that they should remain illiterate. Nevertheless the eunuch institution remained an integral pan of the Inner Court, based on the emperor's need of male descendants and his consequent maintenance of a harem. Later emperors grew up in the Inner Court, often personally devoted to eunuchs who had been their childhood companions or preceptors. The eunuchs' ranks and duties proliferated within the palace, and their influence gradually extended into the entire administration. In the 1420's a palace school was set up for them. The number of eunuchs increased to thousands. In a central office in Peking (the Eastern Yard), they kept secret files on official personnel, accessible only to the emperor. They became, in effect, a separate echelon of administration, not unlike a present-day security system. This was be-cause eunuchs, as palace inmates, lacking family loyalties and completely dependent upon their master, had a unique inside position, closer to the imperial person than any of the scholar-officials. Eunuchs consequently gained great influence as trusted agents of the emperor, even becoming commanders of military forces or inspectors in the provinces. The Ming saw a constant struggle for power between the eunuchs and the Grand Secretaries within the palace, and also between these groups of the Inner Court and the top officials of the imperial bureaucracy, or Outer Court, at the capital.

The arbitrariness of the emperor's rule was visibly demonstrated in another custom, the corporal punishment of high officials at the court. Hung-wu had early followed the Mongol precedent of having officials publicly and ceremoniously beaten with the bamboo. He had a dozen officials executed at various times on suspicion of having inserted derogatory puns in their congratulatory memorials. Such treatment contravened the Confucian doctrine that punishments are for the unlettered masses while the superior man is to be moved by the power of the ruler's moral example. The Ming regime, famous for exalting the letter of the Classics, became notorious for contravening their spirit.

Another phenomenon of the Ming court was factionalism. Cliques of officials became violently involved in one dispute after another, hating their opponents, appointing members of their own faction to office when they could, accusing those in power when they were not. However, the unconfined power of the emperor and the factionalism of officials were active mainly at the level of the imperial bureaucracy, which was spread very thinly over the empire. At the local level was a stable social order in which the emperor's power was held in reserve and seldom exercised.

The Structure of Government.   The Ming emperors retained the inherited structure of central government: first, a civil bureaucracy under the Six Ministries and other organs; second, a centralized military hierarchy; and third, a separate hierarchy of censors. In Western eyes the Board of Censors is perhaps the most interesting of the three. Its chief bureau at the capital had a staff of 110 "investigating censors." In addition, each ministry had a special censorial staff that watched its operations. Censors drawn from the general civil were typically younger officials of rather low rank, selected for personal qualities of probity. When sent into the provinces, often on one-year tours of duty, they investigated the conduct of justice and of ceremonies, the condition of granaries and of schools, and received reports from officials and complaints from the public. Their power came from their having direct access to the throne, both to impeach other officials and to remonstrate (at their peril) with the emperor. These broad powers were limited by the fact that censors usually returned to the regular civil bureaucracy after a tenure of nine years or less; like all officials, they depended upon the imperial whim. Protected neither by life tenure nor by immunity from their master's wrath, these "eyes and ears of the emperor" were in reality bureaucrats like all their fellows, concerned for their own safety, dependent upon favorable merit ratings from their superiors, and sometimes open to bribery or intimidation.

This threefold administration of the Ming and Ch'ing has an interesting comparability with the recent regimes of the Kuomintang and the Chinese Communist Party. Since 1928, China has been governed through the three principal echelons of party, army, and government. The modern governing parties in China may be viewed as the successors of the dynastic families, from whom the rulers were chosen and to whom they answered. The party apparatus, running parallel to army and civil administration, has also inherited some of the ancient censorial functions. This Chinese trinity is not a separation or balance of powers, like that under the Constitution of the United States, but perhaps we may call it a system of balanced administration. The military forces kept the regime in power, the civil bureaucracy carried on the government, and the censors (and also the eunuchs) kept watch on everything.

The territorial civil administration of the Ming was divided into 15 provinces, which the Ch'ing later increased, by subdivision, to 18. Each province was divided into local units composed of still smaller prefectures, of which there were, generally speaking, 159 in the Ming Empire; subprefectures or departments, of which there were 234; and counties (hsien), which totalled 1171. Under the Ch'ing these totals expanded to roughly 183 prefectures and 1470 counties (also called districts). The local administrative hierarchy of magistrates, according to the law of avoidance, were never permitted to serve in their own native provinces lest they be seduced into collusion with kinfolk and local friends. These officials in ascending order were the hsien magistrate, the subprefect, and the prefect. Their administration was headed by a provincial administrative commissioner. There was also a judicial commissioner or judge, with his own staff. A third top official was the provincial military commander. Thus each province was under a collegial group of officers who represented the same threefold administrative, military, and supervisory functions as in the capital. A governor was eventually added as a coordinator at the top of each province. The administrative hierarchy was also watched, as already noted, by censors on tour.

The Ming military system developed by Hung-wu was based on guards units of 5600 men. Each unit was divided into five subunits of 1120 men, who were registered professional soldiers. By 1393 there were 493 guards units under the Ministry of War, stationed at strategic spots on the Inner Asian frontier and the seacoast, along the Grand Canal and at the capital, under five main regional commands. The original guards units had thus become garrisons, independent of the local civil administration. The positions of the registered soldiers were hereditary, and many were given land on which to farm for their livelihood, in the hope of realizing the ancient ideal of a self-supporting army of farmer-soldiers. But inevitably, these Chinese garrisons, even more than Khitan, Jurchen, or Mongol troops, found it difficult to remain effective soldiers in a society.

As at the capital, new administrative organs in the provinces began informally and later became institutionalized. Among these were the intendants of circuit (*tao-t'ai,* Anglicized as taotai), first appointed to handle special functions connected with the salt monopoly, police, customs, river conservancy, or the like. Eventually, the provinces were each divided for these various purposes into a number of circuits, which formed a new administrative level between the provincial and the prefectural levels. Another development was the sending of new traveling inspectors and special commissioners from the capital to check corruption and mis-government. Such officials were given certain administrative, censorial, and military powers within designated areas, so as to introduce a more unified executive capacity into the territorial administration. From them developed, by the middle of the Ming era, the office of provincial governor, already mentioned, as well as that of governor-general, an official normally in charge of two provinces.

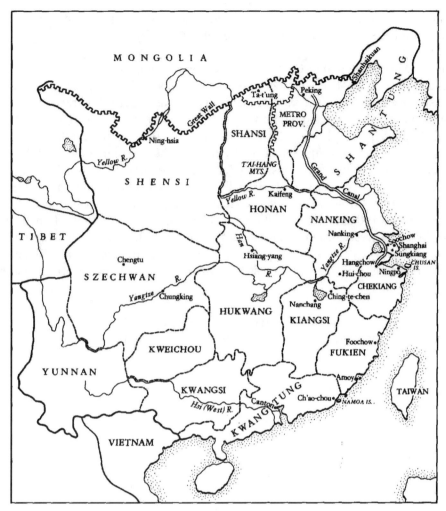

CHINA UNDER THE MING

Land, People, and Taxes. The Ming government's control over the land and the people was signalized by the drawing up of detailed registers of land and of population. In 1393 the population registers gave an estimated total of 10 million households and 60 million persons. This registration, not based on a modern type of census, produced a total no greater than that of the Han period. We can only wonder whether the population in 1393 may not have been double this figure. The land registers in recorded a total of roughly 129 million acres of land in use, less than half the estimated acreage of cultivated land in recent times. Each holding was classified according to type and productivity and was taxed accordingly.

Taxation followed the tradition which went back to the Double Tax of the eighth century (see pages 120-121). The Ming Summer Tax was collected in the eighth month on the supplementary crops grown during the winter and harvested in early summer. The Autumn Grain Tax was collected in the second month on produce grown during the previous summer and harvested in the autumn, above all on the great rice crop of the Yangtze Valley. The usual government monopoly taxes on tea and salt were also maintained. The Ming continued to issue paper money, as the

Sung and Yüan had done, but made it unconvertible into metal currency (copper cash or silver bullion), so that it became worthless and had to be abandoned by 1450.

Households were classified into three, five, or nine grades (there were many complexities) and were obliged to provide labor service according to the number of registered adult males between sixteen and sixty years of age. One kind of labor service was to bear local responsibilities in connection with tax collections and public works. This service was organized under the system. Ideally, each 110 neighboring households formed a unit or village). Within this unit each year one of the ten leading families superintended one-tenth of the 100 remaining households to form a *chia* or section, which bore the responsibility for local labor service during the year. The others served in rotation over a ten-year period. Thus the *li-chia* system had common features with but was separate and distinct from the *pao-chia* system of mutual guarantee which had been inherited from the Sung (pages 100 and 129). Another kind of labor service, also apportioned among the male adults, involved prescribed tasks in the big government offices (*ya-men*, Anglicized as yamen), or else money payments for supplies for the yamen. Still other forms of labor service, apportioned among the populace, required service at the government post stations and in the local militia.

The Ming legal system showed the same pattern of reapplying traditional principles with a new thoroughness. A comprehensive body of administrative and criminal law was first published in 1397.

Yet the early Ming government remained, by modern standards, superficial. It claimed the prerogative of organizing and controlling all aspects of society. But in practice it did not interfere with the Chinese people in their daily lives. There were in the provinces only about two thousand principal posts. If one adds minor incumbents, the total of civil officials in the Ch'ing Empire as late as 1800 was only around twenty thousand. The control of the country by such a small number of mandarins, as Chinese officials came to be called by Westerners, was feasible only because of the functions performed by the dominant elite in each locality, that is, the degree-holders or gentry.

SOCIETY AND CULTURE UNDER THE MING

The Examination System. In the Ming revival of a purely Chinese rule over China, the animating spirit had been to return to the pre-Mongol institutions of the T'ang and Sung. This soon built up the importance of the examination system. Under the Ming and Ch'ing there were three main levels of examination activity: First were preliminary examinations in the county which qualified one to compete in examinations held during two out of every three years at the prefectural city (fu). This gave one the lowest principal degree, that of licentiate or bachelor, called by the ancient name of *hsui-ts'ai*, "flowering talent." This admitted one to the privileged class of literati, who enjoyed exemption from labor service and corporal punishments. In order to retain this lower-gentry status, the holder had to pass routine examinations, usually every three years. For the second level another preliminary test led to the great triennial examinations at the provincial capitals, where thousands of candidates would spend several days incarcerated with brush and paper in the long rows of individual cells at the examination field. One out of every one to two hundred competitors became a provincial graduate or "recommended man" (*chü-jen*), eligible to compete at the third level in the triennial metropolitan examinations at Peking. If successful at the capital, he became a metropolitan graduate or "presented scholar" (*chin-shih*), went to the palace for a final test by the emperor himself, and then received his official ranking and appointment to a post.

The bureaucratic system flexibly permitted some men to advance with-out examination. One means was the inheritance privilege, by which a son of an official of high rank could receive degree status and sometimes even official position in consideration of his father's merit. Another means under the Ming and Ch'ing, as in all previous dynasties, was to let men secure degree status by purchase. This was done by making a contribution to the imperial treasury. Generally the purchaser was allowed to obtain only degree status, not an actual official post. This admitted him to the gentry class, but not into officialdom. Thus degrees acquired by purchase, clearly designated as such, admitted certain men of wealth, mostly merchants or landlords, to the scholarly elite, giving them, in return for their payments, a qualified recognition within a framework that still gave the genuine scholar the highest prestige. The sale of degree status in this fashion was partly a safety valve, letting ambitious nonintellectuals into the establishment, and partly a source of revenue, which tempted a dynasty particularly in time of need. In the nineteenth century roughly a third of the lowest level degree-holders got them by purchase.

Generally speaking, the examination system brought in the great bulk of the bureaucracy and succeeded in recruiting the best talent of the country for government service. Quotas limited the number who could succeed in each county and province, so as to ensure geographical repre-sentation. Candidates' papers were sometimes copied, without their names, before being read in order to ensure anonymity and impartiality. For the provincial examinations, the examiners were sent out from the capital. The system was managed by the Ministry of Rites, instead of the Ministry of Personnel which supervised the officials' later careers. All these practices ensured the impartial universality of the selection process.

One weakness of the system was its restriction of subject matter to the Four Books, which had been selected as the essence of Confucianism in the Sung, and the Five Classics, again as interpreted by the Sung scholars of the school of Chu Hsi (see pages 149-150). In its passion for formal organization, the Ming adopted finally in 1487 a set form for writing examination papers under eight main headings, with not over seven hundred characters in all and with much use of balance and antithesis. This was the famous "eight-legged essay" style, later denounced as imposing a tyranny of literary structure over thought.

The institutions which prepared examination candidates included so-called government schools, which were ordered to be set up at the county and prefectural levels. But their chief function was to enroll the scholars and hold periodical examinations, not to provide organized instruction or residence facilities. The actual preparation of scholars began in the family or sometimes in a clan school. This gave the advantage to youths from extended families that could afford tutors, specifically from scholar-official families, in which parental example and family tradition provided incentive and guidance.

The chief primer, memorized by many millions during the Ming and Ch'ing eras, was the Three-Character Classic produced in the thirteenth century. It gave in jingle form a concise summary of basic knowledge and doctrine in 356 alternately rhyming lines, each of three characters. The opening lines, when understood, convey the prime doctrine of Mencius that human nature is fundamentally good, an idea universally accepted in China, which was to prove a stumbling block to Western missionaries convinced of original sin. Thus the process of elementary learning was at the same time a process of philosophical indoctrination.

Scholarship. At the top of the intellectual pyramid under the Ming stood the Hanlin Academy, a carefully selected body of outstanding metropolitan graduates, who performed important literary tasks for the court. The ethnocentric reaction of the early Ming centered in this citadel of Confucian doctrine. In addition some 300 private academies were founded in various parts of the country, on the model of the Sung, as centers of scholarly study, discussion, and compilation, usually under the patronage of high officials or rich merchants; some also received imperial encouragement: They brought together eminent scholars, students who received free maintenance and tuition, and small libraries. Academies also published scholarly works and stored the wooden printing blocks.

The emperor's sponsorship of letters and the arts was an important means of maintaining his position as head of the Confucian state and culture. This tradition produced in 1407 the great *Encyclopedia of the Yung-lo Period* in 11,095 volumes—a compilation of all the principal

191

THE THREE-CHARACTER CLASSIC (SAN-TZU CHING). *The first page of a a modern edition, with the title of the book at the upper right-hand corner and the text itself starting on the third line. The commentary appears in smaller type.*

Confucianism and the Succession Crisis of the Wanli Emperor

works on history, government, ethics, geography, etc., inherited from previous ages. Compiled by more than two thousand scholars, it was too large to print. Fewer than four hundred manuscript volumes have survived. The next two centuries saw a continued flood of publication sponsored by the court, by officials, and by academies and families. To try to describe this literature, its great compilations, the myriad monographic treatises, the many genres of belles-lettres, would be no easier than to attempt to describe the literature of all Europe in the same period. To cite one example, after several smaller works had led the way, one scholar (Li spent twenty-six years compiling an illustrated medico which described almost two thousand animal, vegetable, and mineral drugs and gave over eight thousand prescriptions. Completed in it described smallpox inoculation and the uses of mercury, iodine, chaulmoogra oil, ephedrine, and other items of a rich pharmacopoeia upon which the modern world is still drawing. Again, a well-illustrated handbook of industrial technology (by Sung Ying-hsing, printed in 1637; see pages 14, 15, and 74), describes methods and instruments used in producing rice, silk, salt, pottery, metals, coal, paper, weapons, and many other products of China's premodern technology.

The vitality of Ming scholarship reflected processes of social growth of the same sort that had flowered in the Sung. Two centuries of domestic peace under the Ming brought substantial economic growth—big increases in farm production and population as well as in trade and industry. City life flourished accordingly, accompanied by more printing and distribution of books, more widespread education, and a more refined and also more democratized urban culture. Out of this came a larger scholar class as well as an enlarged bureaucracy; yet the problems of Chinese life also proliferated and taxed the powers of Confucian thinkers to maintain an integrated view of society and define the scholar's role in it.

The Ming philosopher most influential on later generations in China and Japan was Wang Yang-ming (1472-1529), a successful high official who went beyond the orthodoxy of Chu His by advocating both spiritual enlightenment through self-examination and a vigorous ethical activism within society. Wang carried further a line of Sung thought (see page 149), the Neo-Confucian school of Idealism or of the Mind which had stemmed from a contemporary of Chu Hsi as a minority school opposed to the dominant Chu Hsi school of Rationalism. In general, this School of the Mind was inclined to deny the dualism of Chu His's system, the sharp distinction between Heaven and man and therefore between "Heavenly Principle" (*t'ien-li*) and "human desire." Instead, it viewed them both as parts of a single realm, which brought it closer to Buddhism. Building on this tradition, Wang Yang-ming's teaching represented a sort of Zen revolt within Confucianism: it put greater stress on meditation and intuitive knowledge. Chu Hsi's interpretation of the classical phrase (from the Great Learning) about the "extension of knowledge through the investigation of things" could thus be revised. Wang advocated instead "the extension of intuitive knowledge," which could be achieved through the investigation of one's own inner mind, the *li* within one. The process for doing this, as in Zen Buddhism, was essentially meditation, leading to a sort of enlightenment. But Confucian self-cultivation sought to eliminate not all desires, as in a Buddhist nonattachment to the world, but only selfish desires, the better to achieve one's dutiful harmony with others and with all creation. This led Wang to stress the "unity of knowledge and conduct." As he put it, is the beginning of conduct; conduct is the completion of knowledge." This has remained a Chinese and Japanese ideal down to the present day.

The Gentry Class. The metropolitan graduates totaled only 25,000 men during the whole Ming period. But the degree-holders of the lower ranks probably numbered at any one time about half a million. These degree-holders of all ranks have been known in Chinese as "officials and scholars" (*shen-shih*). In English the term gentry has been applied to them, but this term requires careful definition. It is ambiguous, for it is applied both to individuals and to families, and may have either a political-social or an economic connotation. Strictly defined, the gentry were individual degree-holders. Yet in China where the family overshadowed the individual, the existence of gentry families (i.e., families that had members who were degree-holders) was to be expected. Individuals became gentry by securing degrees. Yet, in a crowded society based on farming, where landowning was a chief economic support for scholarly study, landlord-gentry families were very common. Degree-holders and landlords overlapped to a considerable but imprecise extent.

GENTRY IDEALS. *From an eighteenth-century work* (Pin-feng hang-i) *illustrating the rewards virtue. The caption (not shown) for the illustration on the left says: "In the tenth month winter cold sets in. The diligent have ample food and feast with wine, play games, and entertain relatives. Parents live in comfort while sons pursue learning." The illustration on the right is for the eleventh month and shows a winter scene. Within their apartments women who have done their weaving sit warmly clothed around a brazier enjoying wine. On the street people who have been indolent suffer from the cold.*

The peculiar strength of Confucian government lay in the fact that the gentry performed so many public functions in the local community without official remuneration. They commonly lived in their big houses in the market towns but also maintained contacts or establishments in the administrative cities. As men of influence, they assumed responsibility for many activities which today are performed by officials. They raised funds for and supervised public works, such as the building and maintenance irrigation ditches and canals with their dikes and dams, and roads with their bridges and ferries. They took responsibility for public morals, maintaining the local Confucian temples and ceremonies. They supported schools and academies. They compiled the local histories or gazetteers. In time of plenty they sponsored orphanages and care for the aged. In time of disaster they provided relief. In the face of disorder, they might get permission to organize local militia as defense forces. In most of these activities they received official encouragement or recognition but not specific appointment to office or any pay. A loose comparison might be made with other classes that have functioned in very different societies, such as the equestrian order of ancient Rome, the modern American business class, or other nonofficial groups that have provided local community leadership.

The interest of the government was to maintain morale and a type of public spirit among the gentry, as opposed to selfish opportunism. To this end the Confucian doctrines were recited in the local Confucian temples and the Son of Heaven issued his exhortations. The six imperial injunctions of Hung-wu were ordered posted in villages in 1397. These said, in effect, "Be filial, be respectful to elders and ancestors, teach your children, and peacefully pursue your livelihood." Thus the great tradition of learning, under the patronage of the head of the state? was used to indoctrinate the common people, while the gentry class as the local elite in turn provided leadership in the orderly life of the villages. Though not aristocratic in a hereditary sense, this was indeed an elitist system, for the degree-holders with their immediate families formed certainly no more than 2 per cent of the population but held the highest social authority outside the small official class itself.

FOREIGN RELATIONS

The Tribute System. Upon gaining the throne, Hung-wu immediately tried to re-establish the grand design of the Chinese state in his foreign relations as well as at home. He sent envoys to the peripheral states, Korea, Japan, Annam (Vietnam), Champa, Tibet, and others, announcing his accession. Tribute missions came from these states and from others to which Mongol expeditions had been sent almost a century earlier, on the established routes of China's overseas trade.

The suzerain-vassal relationship between the ruler of China and rulers of other countries expressed the traditional in which China was assumed to be not only the largest and oldest among the states of the world but indeed their parent and the source of their civilization. Tribute relations involved not only performance of the kowtow, the "three kneelings and nine prostrations," but also many other aspects of interstate relations: the exchange of envoys and conduct of diplomatic relations, repatriation and extradition of persons, regulation of Sino-foreign trade, and special Chinese efforts at self-defense through intimidating, cajoling, or subsidizing foreign tribes and rulers. In short, the fitting of foreign potentates into a hierarchy of superior and inferior, and the expression of this in ritual observances, was merely an extension to the outer world of the "Confucian" social order which the ruler of China sought to maintain at home. The vassal king was given an official patent of appointment and a seal to use on his memorials, which were to be dated by the Chinese ruler's year period. The Son of Heaven affected a paternal interest in the orderly government of the tributary state, confirming the succession of new rulers, sometimes offering military protection against attack, usually conferring the boon of trade with China, and in any case sending down moral homilies and exhortations. This was not an aggressive imperialism. Rather, it was a defensive expression of foreign rulers, if they wished contact with the Middle Kingdom, had to accept its terms and acknowledge the universal supremacy of the Son of Heaven. Trade with China might be of great value. Tribute formalities were the price to be paid. Like so many grand designs, this one failed of perfect execution. Yet Chinese chroniclers, by maintaining the forms of tribute at least in the record, made it seem important. It was often regarded quite differently by the tributaries.

The tribute system served many purposes. To get the "king of Japan" to curb Japanese pirates who were raiding Chinese ports, Hung-wu sent three missions to Japan in 1369-1372, using various repatriation of captured pirates, threatening rescripts from himself, and Chinese monks as envoys, but all to no avail. Japanese piracy continued. Though tribute missions came, they were not always submissive, nor were they from the Japanese sovereign. "You stupid eastern barbarians!" wrote Hung-wu to the Ashikaga shogun, the feudal ruler of Japan. "Living so far across the sea.. .you are haughty and disloyal; you permit your subjects to do evil." The Japanese replied in kind: "Heaven and Earth are vast; they are not monopolized by one ruler."
The high point of tributary activity under Yung-lo saw a brief period of professed Japanese fealty to China, expressed in very dutiful terms but regarded by the Japanese feudal rulers as merely a means of monopolizing the lucrative Chinese trade for themselves. Yung-lo in 1403 reopened the three Superintendencies of Merchant Shipping in the southern coastal provinces, which had been closed in 1374, and built hostels at each to entertain tribute envoys. Japanese missions now came annually for several years. In the usual fashion the Chinese court prepared a series of numbered paper passport tallies, tore them from their stub books, and sent them to the vassal ruler, retaining the stub books. When a mission came to the designated Chinese port to bring tribute and to trade, its ships, goods and persons were all specifically limited by statute. They were recorded on one of the numbered tallies, which could be verified by its fitting into the stub books. Thus all envoys were given bona fides, and imposters were checked. The Japanese shogun could maintain his trade monopoly and the Chinese could identify pirates. Between 1433 and 1549, eleven large Japanese missions, usually of several hundred persons, came to the Chinese court under the tally system, by way of Ningpo. Innumerable problems, arose—rivalry in Japan to get possession of the official tallies, conflicts in China with disorderly Japanese warriors, prolonged haggling at Peking over the prices to be paid for trade goods, which included copper ore and sulphur by the hundreds of tons and Japanese swords by the thousand. Members of missions also carried their own goods for private trade. In addition, they received gifts from the emperor, as did the shogun, in lavish quantity.

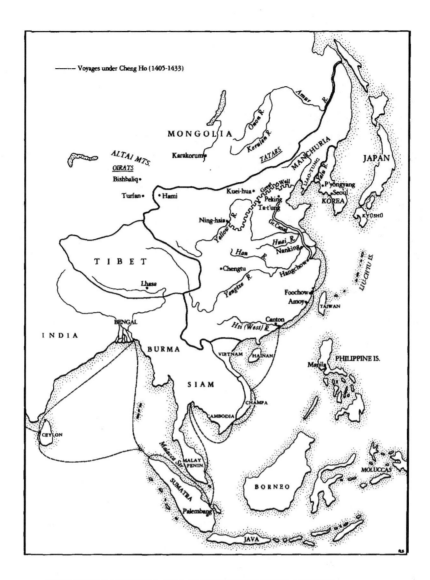

THE MING EMPIRE AND ITS FOREIGN RELATIONS

The Maritime Expeditions. One of Yung-lo's major undertakings was to incorporate the states of South and Southeast Asia into the tribute system. While his motives still remain a matter of speculation, this ambitious venture was marked by seven great maritime expeditions which were begun in 1405, and continued until 1433. They were led for the most part by a Muslim court eunuch named Cheng Ho, who came originally from Yunnan and as a Muslim was well fitted to deal with the Islamic rulers of South Asia. (See map, pages 172-173.) The first fleet sailed in 1405-1407 with sixty-two vessels carrying 28,000 men, and reached India, as did also the second and third. The fourth voyage in reached Aden and the head of Asian circumnavigation at Hormuz on the Persian Gulf. A fifth voyage also went as far as Aden. The seventh voyage started out with 27,500 men and reached Hormuz again in 1431-1433. Chinese vessels visited far down the east coast of Africa, where chinaware and copper cash had been known for centuries. Seven Chinese reached Mecca.

The world had never seen such large-scale feats of seamanship. These Chinese armadas sailed all across the Indian Ocean almost a century before the Portuguese in 1498 reached India by sailing around Africa, and a century and a half before the Spanish Armada of 1588 made Western history by its short voyage around England. Cheng Ho's voyages were made possible by the development of Chinese shipbuilding and techniques of navigation on the Asian sea routes. His seagoing junks were of considerable size, some over four hundred feet in length, with four decks and up to a dozen watertight compartments. They navigated by detailed sailing directions and also used the compass. These remarkable expeditions penetrated to the sources of China's maritime trade not only along the Southeast Asian coasts but also in Ceylon, on both coasts of southern India, and in the Middle East and East Africa. In addition to customary tributaries, like Vietnam and Siam, some fifty new places were visited, and their rulers enrolled as tributaries. Missions from Hormuz and the African coast came to China four times, from Bengal eleven times. Rulers in Sumatra and Ceylon were brought back by force. Back also came ostriches, zebras, and giraffes, the latter touted as the auspicious "unicorn" of Chinese fable.

These spectacular maritime expeditions expressed the exuberance of an era of great vitality. For the eunuch leaders, they brought adventure, fame, and presumably profit. Commercial interests were also no doubt at work on the well-established routes of earlier trade, where Chinese migration had already created large overseas Chinese communities in Southeast Asian ports. Another motive seems to have been broadly political, to bring all the known world within the Chinese tributary scheme of places trading by land were regularly enrolled as tributaries. Why not those trading by sea? This grandiose concept had been in the minds of Mongol emperors and was implicit in the idea of the universal rule of the Son of Heaven.

Speculation as to the causes of the Ming expeditions raises the question of why they were suddenly stopped and never resumed or imitated later. One reason for their cessation was their great cost, at a time when the early Ming campaigns against the Mongols and the building of Peking had begun to deplete the imperial coffers. The great fleets could be criticized as expensive adventures, largely unproductive except for pageantry and strange tales. They were also promoted particularly by court eunuchs, whose activities were opposed by the scholar-officials—so much so that Cheng-Ho's feats were practically suppressed in the historical record.

These demonstrations of the early Ming capacity for maritime expansion were all the more dramatic because Chinese ideas of government and official policies were fundamentally indifferent, if not actually opposed, to such an expansion. The contrast between capacity and performance, if looked at by our modern world of trade and overseas expansion, is truly striking. Chinese seapower, based upon the fishing fleets and trading junks of Canton, Amoy, and Ningpo, had been steadily increasing. China was on the verge of becoming a naval power that could dominate East Asia. The Ming fleets were developing the nautical and logistic capacity to bring military force and trading goods in overwhelming volume to any point in the Eastern seas. But after 1433 this beginning was cut short. No Henry the Navigator came to the Chinese throne. The Ming court, unlike that of contemporary Portugal, had no sustained interest in seafaring, no grasp of the possibilities of seapower. The Ming voyages were not followed up but remained isolated *tours de force*, mere exploits.

Ming Anticommercialism. This contrast throws light on the nature of Chinese society. Cheng Ho lived and sailed a century and a half before Sir Francis Drake and the other captains of Queen Elizabeth began to lay the foundations of the British Empire. The Chinese Empire was then greater than all of Europe in size and in the of her domestic, if not also her foreign, commerce. Yet Ming China, having shown her capacity to do so, failed to become a maritime power. Through this default, the Eastern seas and even the China coast soon came to be dominated by a succession of non-Chinese seafaring peoples-the Japanese, the Portuguese and Spanish, the Dutch, and finally the British and Americans. Out of this commercial and naval domination of East Asian waters emerged eventually those forces of imperialistic expansion which finally humbled the traditional Chinese Empire and led to its disintegration. Cheng Ho, as a court eunuch and high dignitary, lacked precisely those motives which later inspired the merchant-adventurers of Europe. His power and advancement, even as he cruised the Indian Ocean, still depended upon the emperor. Cheng Ho was an organizer, a commander, a diplomat, and an able courtier, but he was not a trader. No chartered companies grew out of his expeditions, empowered like the Virginia Company or the East India Company to found colonies or establish governments overseas. The migration of Chinese into Southeast Asia was already under way, and the Chinese in that area would always outnumber the Europeans who might come there. But the Chinese state remained uninterested in these commercial and colonial possibilities overseas. The Ming and Ch'ing governments got their major sustenance from the land tax, not from trade taxes. They refused to join in the great commercial revolution which was beginning to sweep the world.

To understand this anticommercialism we may suggest several approaches, institutional, economic, ideological, and strategic. The institutional explanation goes back to the early environment of ancient China on the North China Plain far from the sea, where the official class came into being as tax-gatherers, fostering agriculture and gathering its products to maintain themselves and the state. In this agrarian-bureaucratic society merchants were kept subordinate to officialdom and utilized by it. The economic interests that did grow up were centered in domestic, not foreign, commerce simply because the Chinese subcontinent, then as now, was so relatively self-sufficient. But after the growth of commerce during the T'ang, Sung, and why did the Ming and Ch'ing governments revert to the traditional agrarian-centered attitudes of an earlier era? Perhaps one reason was the culturalism we have already mentioned, in particular the establishment of the Neo-Confucian orthodoxy as the matrix of Ming thought. This revived the classical values, including the ancient disesteem of commerce. Foreign trade was left to powerful eunuchs, which made it all the more distasteful to the official class. Another explanation was pre-sumably strategic-the Ming determination to prevent a repetition of the Mongol conquest.

The Mongol Problem. Hung-wu's preoccupation with breaking the Mongol power remained the chief focus of early Ming foreign relations. His aim was not to subjugate the whole of Mongolia but rather to destroy the unity of the tribes, which gave them their striking power. Even before China had been unified, Ming armies crossed the steppe to break up the Mongol forces, twice seizing Mongol chieftains pacified by defeat, intimidation, purchase, or other means were put in charge of Mongol settlements on the border and given titles, honors, emoluments, and opportunities for trade. Using a divide-and-rule policy, the Chinese tried to keep the seminomads of Inner Mongolia as border allies against the fully nomadic and mobile tribes of Outer Mongolia.

In the Central Asian khanate of Chaghadai, the last great successor of Chinggis, the conquerer Timur, known to Europe as Tamerlane (1336-1405), rose to power in 1369. From his capital of Samarkand, he expanded violently in all directions, overrunning Persia and Mesopotamia, defeating the Golden Horde in southern Russia, even briefly invading northern India. Tamerlane had some contact with the Chinese court and conceived the ambition to take it over. When he died in 1405, he had a vast army already on the way eastward to conquer China and make it an Islamic state. His death, however, marked the end of the Mongol era, particularly of the Mongol capacity to keep Central Asia united and so to threaten the agricultural civilizations that bordered on it. The end of a united Central Asia also diminished the trade and contact across it between East and West. Under the Ming and Ch'ing, this land route was severed, and the tribes of Mongolia became more dependent on trade with China alone.

By the early fifteenth century the Mongol tribes were split (see map, page 196): in eastern Mongolia were the Tatars (*Ta-tan* in Chinese, corrupted by Europeans to "Tartars"), in western Mongolia, the Oirats. Chinese strategy was to play each off against the other. The Yung-lo emperor rose to power by leading expeditions against the Mongols and also by finding allies among them on the border. After his usurpation in 1403, Yung-lo personally led five expeditions far out across the steppe. In 1410 he mobilized over 100,000 men with 30,000 cartloads of supplies, overawed the Oirats, gave them gifts and secured their neutrality, crossed the Kerulen River, and defeated the Tatars. However, when the Oirats expanded eastward in 1414, Yung-lo led an army back to the Kerulen and this time defeated the Oirats. Both these Ming expeditions used cannon. Soon the Tatars ventured to raid the border. In 1422 Yung-lo led forth another host of 235,000 men with a supply train of 117,000 carts and 340,000 donkeys. The Tatars escaped westward, however, and further campaigns in 1423 and 1424 were unable to catch them.

Already Yung-lo's removal of the capital in 1421 from Nanking to Peking had symbolized the Ming preoccupation with defense against the Mongols. Imperial strategy centered on the frontier, where Peking stands guard near the principal gateway (the Nan-k'ou Pass) leading from Mongolia down onto the North China Plain. The capital of the great Ming Empire thus was located a scant miles from the traditional northern boundary of China, the Great Wall. This site has been used by dynasties oriented toward Inner Asia-the Liao, Yuan, Ming, and Ch'ing, as well as the Chinese People's Republic since 1949. Southern capitals have been used by regimes originating in the south or oriented toward overseas trade-Hangchow under the Southern Sung; Nanking in the early Ming, under the Taiping rebels and under the Nationalist Government after 1927. Peking was far from the centers of Chinese population and production. Its strategic vulnerability to nomad inroads and its dependence on grain shipments from the lower via the Grand Canal, are startling facts-too startling to be mere accidents. The explanation is that the capital of China had to serve also as the capital of the non-Chinese areas of Inner Asia. The "barbarians" were a constant military and therefore political component of the Chinese Empire; its capital was drawn outward to the border of China as a result.

The Ming expeditions to chastise the Mongols had been part of the effort to keep them harmless by carrot-and-stick methods. The Oirats, for example, had established tribute relations in 1408 and sent missions almost every year, which became a thinly veiled means of keeping them pacified through subsidies, a sort of tribute in reverse. Their annual missions to Peking sometimes totaled two or three thousand persons, including several hundred merchants from Central Asia. Passing through the Great Wall at Ta-t'ung in northern Shansi, this host had to be quartered and banqueted by the local authorities, for, like cultural delegations invited to Peking today, tribute missions were guests of the Middle Kingdom. As tribute, the Oirats presented their chief native product, horses, and received in return imperial "gifts in reply," mainly silk and satin textiles. A few days of free trade in the market followed the presentation of tribute within the Forbidden City. In this context of profitable exchange, the "barbarians" acquiesced in the "three kneelings and nine prostrations" as a traditional court ceremony. While gaining the nomads' submission, China had to suffer their depredations on the route between the border and the capital, and their drunken roistering at Peking. For the Mongols, the trip spelled glamour and profit, from fees paid them by the Muslim traders to whom their tribute missions gave cover. Many bearers of "tribute" were actually merchants claiming to represent distant and sometimes nonexistent potentates. The Ming *Collected Statutes* listed thirty-eight countries of the Western Regions which submitted tribute by way of Hami, the natural funnel for the caravan trade. Among them, for example, the Kingdom of Rum in Asia Minor (i.e., the long defunct Roman East) was recorded as presenting tribute as late as 1618. The Ming viewed this thin trickle of Central Asian tributary trade as having political rather than fiscal value, as it kept troublesome warriors quiet on the frontier.

In the late 1430's, just as the overseas expeditions came to an end, the Inner Asian frontier saw a violent recrudescence of the Mongol threat. A new chieftain of the Oirats subjugated then extended his influence over the tribes to the east all the way to Korea, and in late 1449 mobilized his horde along the border, threw off the forms of tribute, and approached Ta-t'ung. The Ming emperor, a product of palace life, was under the ill-advised domination of his chief eunuch, who took the emperor into the field and foolishly advanced toward Ta-t'ung to do battle. The Oirats advanced, defeated, pursued, and destroyed the Chinese force, and captured the emperor. But when they came to Peking, they found that the war minister and others had prepared a defense with cannon, enthroned a new emperor, and affected no interest in the former one. After several days before the walls, the Oirats went back to Mongolia. Next year they sent back the useless emperor and soon resumed their profitable tribute relations.

Ming-Mongol relations during the next century were a mixture of border raids and tribute missions. In 1550 a new leader, Altan Khan of the eastern Mongols, united a large striking force, came through the Wall from the northeast, and pillaged around Peking again for several days before withdrawing. Ming defenses of walls, beacon towers, and military agricultural colonies on the frontier were offset by Chinese deserters who aided the raiders. Such Chinese helped Altan Khan try to establish a settled administration. He built a capital city at Kuei-hua outside the Wall, northwest of Ta-t'ung. Eventually in the 1570's he was pacified and given the hopeful title of "Obedient and Righteous Prince" (Shun-i Wang). Until the rise of the Manchu Empire, however, Mongol booting continued to harass the Chinese border.

Troubles with Japan. From the cost of the Japanese and the Mongol tribute missions, we can see why the Ming court may have preferred to let the tribute system rest in comparative abeyance overseas after the first half of the fifteenth century. The expense of maintaining, transporting, and bestowing gifts upon hundreds of functionaries and merchants who came to Peking was not compensated by the trade they conducted. Missions from Southeast Asia grew fewer and fewer. The Islands alone remained a regular maritime tributary on a biennial basis, serving actually as an indirect channel for Sino-Japanese trade. In this context of fading grandeur and frontier disorder, the first Europeans to reach China by sea, Portuguese adventurers in 1514, seemed to the Chinese only a small increment in a general growth of piracy and unwanted relations on the China coast.

In Japan a growing maritime capacity had produced overseas adventurers a full century before the Elizabethan age glorified the somewhat com-parable exploits of gentleman-pirates from England. Like Drake and Hawkins, the Japanese could trade or loot by turns, as opportunity offered. Their bigger ships could carry three hundred men. Landing suddenly and attacking villages with their great swords, the pirates would seize pro-visions, hostages, and loot and make their getaway. Although known in Chinese records as "Japanese pirates" (*Wo-k'ou*, or in Japanese, *Wakō*, a term with pejorative connotations of "dwarf"), these raiders actually included many Chinese. Unlike the Mongol raids, the disloyal Chinese in these forays were not so much advisers as principal participants. By the latter decades of Ming rule, Chinese actually formed the majority among the "Japanese pirates."

The Ming response to this growing disorder, the prohibition of maritime trade, reflected the court's agrarian-minded and land-based unconcern for foreign commerce in general. The prohibition had the effect of forcing crews and captains into smuggling or buccaneering for a livelihood. Pirate raids after 1550 became actual invasions. The pirates based themselves on Chusan Island south of Shanghai, which was later to be the British base in 1840, and in 1552 they attacked inland cities in Chekiang, while others went up the Yangtze. In defense, Ming pirate-suppressors bought over the leading renegades with rewards and pardons and attacked the pirate lair on Chusan. But the scourge increased. Japanese harassment of the South China coast declined only with the political reunification of Japan in the late sixteenth century. However, this reunification concentrated Japan's military energies in a form even more menacing and exhausting to the Ming court.

Peking learned of Japan's intent to invade China by way of Korea through spies in Japan as well as from Korea. In 1592, when the Japanese attack on Korea came, the court debated whether to send a fleet from the southern provinces to attack Japan, or to put an army on the Korean frontier, or to negotiate for peace. In the end the court decided it had to fulfill its suzerain duty to aid Korea in order to defend Southern Manchuria and North China. Ming forces did not cross the Yalu until after the whole peninsula was in Japanese hands. The Chinese attacked Pyongyang in mid 1592, were badly defeated, and started negotiations to gain time. Early in 1593 they surprised the Japanese, drove them out of Pyongyang, and advanced to the outskirts of the capital, Seoul, but were ambushed and again defeated. The short swords of the Chinese cavalry proved no match for the long swords, spears, and guns of the Japanese infantry. Negotiations and exhausting conflict continued until the Japanese finally withdrew in 1598 (after a second invasion in force in 1597). The total Ming expenditure to meet the first Japanese invasion of Korea must have come to over 10 million taels, with a comparable sum required later to meet the second invasion. The administration was already close to bankruptcy, after constant subsidies to the Mongols and rebuilding of Peking palaces. Japan's invasions of Korea were a final strain on Peking's dwindling resources and prepared the way for the rise, after 1600, of bandits within and "barbarian" invaders from without.

THE MING ECONOMY

Economic Growth. In studying China's economic history, we must constantly distinguish between the imperial regime and the country as a whole. We have noted the court's anticommercial attitude and approach to final bankruptcy. But if we look at the late Ming economy as a whole, we find much evidence of growth in almost all its aspects-population, area of cultivated land, volume of foreign trade, production of handicraft and industrial goods, and even, perhaps, in the use of money.

Tax grain (called by Western writers "tribute rice") had to be trans-ported from the rice baskets of the Huai River and lower Yangtze to feed the new capital at Peking. Sea transport around Shantung was increasingly hindered by Japanese pirates, and was in any case expensive. Yung-lo therefore dug out the unused "Connecting Canal" in western Shantung that Khubilai Khan had first constructed as part of the second Grand Canal system, and installed fifteen locks. Three thousand or more shallow boats were now used on the canal route, and after 1415 sea transport was given up. But transport of tax grain to collecting depots on the canal, still part of the labor-service obligation of the peasantry, became a heavy burden on them. Yung-lo's successors therefore placed the task of transportation entirely on certain military transport divisions of the local garrisons, which had to be increased from 120,000 to 160,000 men. From the 1430's this new system supplied usually over 3 million Chinese bushels (say roughly 200,000 tons), and sometimes over 5 million, to the capital every year.

Trade between North and South China was stimulated by the growth of Peking and the canal system. Trade on the Yangtze and in South China also increased. For example, merchants in the southernmost part of modern Anhwei spread their operations widely into other provinces. Called, from an old place name, merchants," they traded in all manner of com-modities-porcelains from the nearby production center at Ching-te-chen in Kiangsi, teas and silks locally produced, salt, timber, and comestibles. Naturally they developed the close relations with officialdom that such extensive operations required for their protection.

Specialized handicraft production grew up for this enlarging market and even some larger-scale manufacturing. At Ching-te-chen the imperial kilns produced great quantities of porcelain for the palace and also for upper-class use and even for export. The particular clay now known as kaolin (named for *Kao-ling*, "High Ridge," a hill east of Ching-te-chen; a hydrous silicate of alumina), when properly prepared with other substances and heated to about 1400 degrees Centigrade, becomes white, translucent, and so hard that steel will not scratch it. This porcelain was a truly superior product in the eyes of Europeans, who lacked the technique and who properly called it "chinaware." Again, Soochow became a national center of trade, finance, and processing industries, particularly the weaving and dyeing of silk. The nearby Sungkiang region, inland from Shanghai, became a late Ming center for cotton cloth production, using raw cotton from other provinces both north and south, and sending its product back for sale there. Canton iron pans (shallow cooking pans for use directly over fire) were exported widely throughout China, overseas, and to Central Asia.

This domestic commercial growth led to the setting up in the sixteenth century of numerous regional guilds with guild halls in major centers, especially Peking. These bodies were created chiefly by officials and merchants who came from a common region—a province, prefecture, county, or city—so as to have a convenient center of contact and mutual aid in a distant place, preeminently at the capital.

Meanwhile China's maritime trade developed steadily in the late Ming outside the framework of the tribute system. Missions from Southeast and South Asia became fewer, while Chinese merchants who went overseas became more numerous . In short, foreign trade was no longer brought to China principally by intermediaries, like the Arabs, but was now carried by Chinese merchants who went abroad with Chinese products and on their return with foreign wares entered easily into the stream of China's wise junk traffic. The government did little to encourage this trade and sometimes banned it, but it continued to grow.

The Single-Whip Reform. The traditional taxes on land and labor underwent a gradual reform during the sixteenth century, which reduced them to money payments and simplified them by combining many small items into one. The whole movement has become known as the "Single-Whip" reform. (The name is a pun, since meaning "combination in one item," sounds also like "a single whip.")

The evils in the land and labor taxes had begun with the falsification of local records. As we have seen on pages 186-187, both landholdings and households early in the Ming period were classified into grades and remained supposedly subject to reclassification every ten years or so. Each man's tax burden depended first of all on his classification in the local registers. But responsibility for management of the system was placed on the leading households—the wealthier families, who thus had an opportunity to escape their allotted burden by falsifying the records. By collusion and bribery, these interested parties could reduce their own tax liability, providing they could increase that of the poorer households to meet the overall tax quota of the area. Many methods could be used: concealing the number of male adults, removing land from the record altogether, registering land under the name of a servant or tenant, or registering private land as government land or private persons as officials. Because of the special privileges enjoyed by wealthier families, smaller households often sought their protection, transferring the nominal ownership of their land in order to escape the tax burden, for a consideration paid privately to the large household. As a result, the official registers within a few generations became meaningless, while taxation became chaotic-a racket levied by the powerful upon the weak. Revenue collections ran short, the government above suffered loss, and the poorer peasants beneath were milked harder than ever, while the large households and petty officials in between benefited from their mutual arrangements. Since this middle stratum of leading families in the countryside provided many of the holders through examination or purchase, they became all the more a "landlord-gentry" ruling class.

The confusion of this situation was compounded by the variety of taxes. The forms of landholding were complex: rights to the subsoil might be held by one person but rights to the use of the surface by another, who might lease the use of the surface to a tenant, who could sublet in turn. Tenantry assumed many forms. The labor service charges became even more complex. They were apportioned on the basis of a factor less stable than land, namely, the number of male adults, and might vary according to local needs and by decision of the local powerholders. As the institution became more corrupt, demands for labor services bore so hard on the poorer peasantry that first households, then sections (*chia*) of villages, and finally whole villages (*li*) began to abscond. Since tax quotas were seldom diminished, this increased still further the burden on those left behind. Finally, as more and more items became commuted to money payments, the tax collectors had every opportunity to add surtaxes and extra fees, commute labor into silver inequitably, and maintain assessments after the need for the original services had passed. The result was a limitless web of money taxes entangling the peasantry, levied in all seasons of the year for myriad nominal or alleged purposes, inequitably assessed and imperfectly recorded, according to no general scheme and under no superior control or direction.

The Single-Whip reform was carried out gradually by many hard-pressed provincial officials in one area after another, in a desperate effort to maintain a reliable tax structure and regular collections. It occurred chiefly in the period 1522-1619, that is, in the final century of effective Ming administration. It consisted of two principal tendencies-to combine all the various items of taxation under one or a few headings and to collect them in silver. One basic reform was to simplify the land classification so that in place of as many as a hundred different land tax rates, there were only two or three rates. Another reform was to unify the land taxes, combining sometimes thirty or forty different taxes into two or three items. Labor services were similarly unified. Next, the two major categories of land tax and labor service were sometimes combined to make a single item. Finally, dates of collection were unified, as well as the apparatus for it, which reduced the opportunities for extortion and fraud.

The resulting fiscal situation was probably no simpler than it would be to have a separate income tax law for each county in the United States. The Single-Whip reform was only a partial step toward a modernized tax structure. After the reform, the government used its tax receipts in silver to pay wages to hired laborers, who performed the labor service tasks formerly required of the common people. Communities were no longer required to transport their tax grain to a government granary. The reform also abolished the former indirect payment of taxes through the section and village heads. Instead, the taxpayer now put his tax silver directly into the government collector's silver chest in front of the local yamen and got an official receipt.

Several earlier dynasties had begun by relying at first on taxes and services in kind, only to have the system deteriorate, until a reform simplified it by a greater recourse to tax collections in money. In the late Ming this increased use of money was related to the vigorous economic growth already mentioned and in particular to the inflow of silver from abroad.

THE END OF MING RULE

Even if we make allowance for human frailty among historians-their capacity to find in the voluminous record of history the evidence they may seek for almost any interpretation of events-still the drama of the late Ming has all the classic features of a dynastic decline: effete and feckless rulers, corrupt favorites misusing their power, factional jealousies among officials, fiscal bankruptcy, natural disasters, the rise of rebellion and, finally, foreign invasion. These evils in the last decades of Ming rule were highlighted by the fact that they followed a vigorous reform effort under Chang Chü-cheng, one of the great ministers of the era, who rose to supreme power as senior Grand Secretary during the first decade (1573-1582) of the Wan-li reign. Chang was on good terms with the Outer Court and influential with the young emperor. He tried to increase the land tax revenue by getting exempted lands taxed again. He tried to restrict the ever-growing perquisites and privileges of the official class and the imperial family. Yet Chang, for all his efforts, could not check the emperor's greed. After his death in 1582, Wan-li, reigning for another thirty-eight years until 1620, became utterly irresponsible. He avoided seeing his ministers for years on end, refused to conduct business or make needed appointments, let evils flourish, and squandered the state's resources. The fifteen-year-old emperor who ascended the throne in 1620 was a dim-wit interested mainly in carpentry. He let his nurse's close friend, the eunuch Wei Chung-hsien who had been butler in his mother's apartments, take over the government. Wei brought the eunuch evil to its highest point. Backed by a small eunuch army to control the palace and a network of spies throughout the empire, he recruited unprincipled opportunists among the bureaucracy, purged his enemies in official life, and levied extortionate new taxes in the provinces.

Factionalism: The Tung-Lin Party. The Confucian resistance to these evils was carried on mainly by a group of scholars, whose long struggle and eventual failure make a poignant chapter in the annals of Chinese politics. Tung-lin (literally, "Eastern Forest") was the name of an academy at at Wusih on the lower Yangtze. Led by a dozen scholar-ex-officials, most of whom had been dismissed during factional controversies at the court, its members lectured at affiliated academies nearby, and soon spread their influence among scholars and officials elsewhere in a moral crusade to reassert the traditional principles of Confucian conduct. They condemned the philosophical eclecticism that had grown popular in the sixteenth century since the time of Wang Yang-ming, and that seemed to confuse Confucianism, Buddhism and Taoism. They stressed the supreme importance of moral integrity and denounced various holders of power, both Grand Secretaries and eunuchs.

The Tung-lin reformers of course had an incomplete monopoly on virtue. By 1610 they were being denounced in turn as a *tang* (the modern word for "party"), that is, an organized clique of the sort traditionally anathematized as subversive of imperial authority and bureaucratic harmony. The factional struggle was conducted in terms less of state policies than of the moral qualities of ministers. Denouncing and being denounced, the Tung-lin crusaders had their ups and downs. They became dominant in the years 1620-1623, just before the eunuch Wei Chung-hsien achieved complete power. In 1624 a Tung-lin leader accused Wei of twenty-four high crimes, including murders and a forced abortion of the empress. Wei mobilized the enemies of the reformers and retaliated with terror. Black-lists were compiled of some seven hundred Tung-lin supporters. Leading figures were denounced, condemned, dismissed, disgraced, imprisoned, tortured, and beaten to death. The Tung-lin group had been practically wiped out by the time Wei fell from power in 1627. This eunuch's manipulation of the sacred office of the Son of Heaven for evil ends had completed the moral degradation of the Ming regime.

The Rise of Rebellion. Yet the Ming collapse was perhaps due less to misgovernment than to nongovernment, less to eunuch immorality than to the regime's failure to keep up with its problems. The real problem was not that tax burdens were oppressive but that tax revenues were inadequate. The administration suffered less from tyranny than from paralysis.

When Shensi in the Northwest was hard hit by famine in 1628, a postal employee named Li Tzu-ch'eng was thrown out of his job by unwise gov-ernment economies. Li joined his uncle, who was already a bandit, and made his lair on the edge of the North China Plain in the mountains southern Shansi, the same area where the Japanese during World War proved unable to dislodge the Chinese irregular forces. Li Tzu-ch'eng raided Honan and Szechwan, acquiring more followers, and eventually some of the forms of an organized government. At least two scholars joined him and advised him how to win popular support. They spread songs and stories about his heroic qualities, helped him distribute food to the starving, appoint officials, proclaim a dynasty, confer titles, and even issue his own coinage. By 1643 Li Tzu-ch'eng held much of Hupei, Honan, and Shensi. Early in 1644 he descended on Peking from the northwest, just as the last Ming emperor hanged himself on Prospect Hill, overlooking the For-bidden City.

Meanwhile Li's chief rival, another rebel named Chang Hsien-chung, had acquired a great reputation more as a killer than as an organizer of men. From about 1630 he had raided widely through North China, plundering with hit-and-run tactics. Finally in 1644 he invaded Szechwan and set up a government, complete with Six Ministries and a Grand Secretariat, headed by genuine metropolitan graduates who held examinations and minted money. But Chang's main concern was stamping out opposition with terror tactics, used especially against the gentry. He lost gentry sup-port, and the Manchus killed him in 1647.

Thus the Ming dynasty was destroyed by Chinese rebels before it was superseded by "barbarian" invaders. But the Manchu conquerors preserved and used the major institutions of government that had functioned for more than two centuries under the Ming. The downfall of Ming rule must therefore be attributed less to the structure of these institutions than to their malfunctioning under the accumulated stresses that typify the end of a dynastic cycle.

Appendix C: Recommended Reading

GENERAL INTEREST

Denis Twitchett and John K. Fairbank, *The Cambridge History of China*, vols. 7-8, The Ming Dynasty, 1368-1644 (1998).
> For further information on topics including government, fiscal administration, law, foreign relations, socio-economic development, and thought the late Ming.

Paul Ropp, *Heritage of China: Contemporary Perspectives on Chinese Civilization* (1990).
> Introductory articles on traditional China, covering government, economics, women and the family, and the Confucian tradition, and so forth.

Albert Chan, *The Glory and Fall of the Ming Dynasty* (1982).
> A general narrative account of the Ming broken up into topics especially relevant to the game (e.g., government, eunuchs, merchants, fiscal administration, taxation, education, conditions in the provinces, rebels, and bandits).

Timothy Brook, *The Confusions of Pleasure: Commerce and Culture in Ming China* (1998).
> A broad narrative of the Ming focusing on commerce but touching on a variety of political and cultural issues that come up in the course of the game.

Robert Crawford, "Chang Chü-cheng's Confucian Legalism," in Wm. Theodore De Bary, et al, *Self and Society in Ming Thought* (1970).

Daniel K. Gardner, *Learning to Be a Sage: Selections from the Conversations of Master Chu, Arranged Topically* (University of California Press, 1990); and *Zhu Xi's Reading of the Analects: Canon, Commentary, and the Classical Tradition (Columbia University Press, 2003).*
> Studies of the "neo-Confucianism" that became orthodoxy in China from the thirteenth century until the early years of the twentieth century.

SPECIALIZED / TOPICAL

You are encouraged to conduct additional research when preparing memorials on specialized topics. For example, you may wish to understand the structure of government, the civil service examination, the financial issues facing the empire, the high degree of factionalism in the bureaucracy, or the central role played by eunuchs during the Ming. Or, you may be interested in pursuing Chinese relations with "pirates" along the Southeast coast, "barbarians" to the north and northwest, and Westerners. Consult the instructor for guidance.